SHARING YOUR
Faith
EFFECTIVELY

SHARING YOUR  EFFECTIVELY

CAMMY WALTERS

TATE PUBLISHING
AND ENTERPRISES, LLC

Sharing Your Faith Effectively
Copyright © 2014 by Cammy Walters. All rights reserved.

No part of this publication may be reproduced, stored in a retrieval system or transmitted in any way by any means, electronic, mechanical, photocopy, recording or otherwise without the prior permission of the author except as provided by USA copyright law.

Scripture taken from the *New King James Version*®. Copyright © 1982 by Thomas Nelson, Inc. Used by permission. All rights reserved.

The opinions expressed by the author are not necessarily those of Tate Publishing, LLC.

Published by Tate Publishing & Enterprises, LLC
127 E. Trade Center Terrace | Mustang, Oklahoma 73064 USA
1.888.361.9473 | www.tatepublishing.com

Tate Publishing is committed to excellence in the publishing industry. The company reflects the philosophy established by the founders, based on Psalm 68:11,
"The Lord gave the word and great was the company of those who published it."

Book design copyright © 2014 by Tate Publishing, LLC. All rights reserved.
Cover design by Gian Philipp Rufin
Interior design by Jake Muelle

Published in the United States of America

ISBN: 978-1-63306-964-0
1. Religion / Christian Education / General
2. Religion / Christian Life / Spiritual Growth
14.08.28

Dedication

First and Foremost, I want to dedicate this book to the Author and Finisher of my faith, Jesus Christ, My Lord, My Savior, and My Best Friend!

Secondly, I dedicate this book to all Christians that struggle to share their Christian faith with others. I pray that through this handbook, you will no longer struggle with your faith, or how to express it!

Thirdly, I want to dedicate this book to Nancy Shoop my editor, and good friend. Without her tireless hours of reading, our many discussions on the topics, and her tenacious kicks to my backside to get this book done it would not have been possible. Please know that without your friendship, support and many long hours spent together, I wouldn't have written anything at all.

Lastly however never least, My Dearest Husband, Don Walters, without his complete and utter confidence in me through whatever situation may arise, embodies the true and pure Love of God. He is truly the best part of me, and without him, I don't know where I would be. I love you baby, and am truly grateful to God that He sent you to me!

Special Acknowledgements

First, I would like to thank my Heavenly Father God for allowing me the privilege to write such a book to help so many Christians share their faith across the globe. Truly, an End-Time endeavor by this 11th hour worker!

Secondly, a special thank you again to Dan and Becky Skelton dba BJs Photographs for providing my author photographs and for being dear and loving friends that God has placed in my life.

Thirdly, a special thank you to all the employees of my publisher Tate Publishing for believing in me as an author, and providing all the time, effort and expense of publishing my work. Each of you in your own way have helped spread and share the gospel of Jesus Christ throughout the world and great will be your reward!

Contents

Introduction 11
Sharing Your Faith with an Unbeliever............. 13
Sharing Your Faith on Water Baptism 25
Assurance of Salvation to All Believers............. 31
Baptism of the Holy Spirit....................... 41
Healing to the Sick............................. 55
Prayer—Talking to Your Father 65
Protecting Our Christian Identity 73
Kingdom Experience 87
Understanding Our Righteousness Through Christ... 93
Overview of the Spiritual Gifts 101
Death Issues................................... 119
Three Dimensions of Covenants 129
The First Dimension of Covenant Agreements 131
    Covenants Between Men 131
The Second Dimension of Covenant Agreements ... 137
    Men with God 137

The Third and Ultimate Dimension of Covenant
    Agreements.............................. 147
  God With Man 147
Covenant Devotional Standing on the Promises of
    God 153
Keeping it Real.............................. 171
About the Author............................ 173

Introduction

Through my teaching the Word of God for the past 25 years, the one thing that seems to confound most Christians is sharing one's faith. This one area seems to be the most difficult and daunting of tasks for most Christians in our society today and really should be the one thing that should come the most naturally to us. Many believe that in order to share one's faith they must have some credentials or badges to backup what they are saying in order for anyone to believe them. This is simply not true, and thus, the reason that I have put together this handbook on how to share your faith. I wanted you to have a complete and concisely written tool, to provide you the confidence that you need to share your faith and present anyone anywhere with thought provoking information and insight into your faith and beliefs.

In this handbook, you will discover that we have covered the most basic of Christian principles in order to assist you in not only explaining your faith, but also explaining it in such a way that others will understand and grasp the same faith and beliefs that you hold so dear. I have also included an introduction to understanding Covenant Agreements toward the end of this book so that they might help develop your own faith and understanding of your faith as you grow and mature into the Christian that God intended you to become. The chapters on covenant will help you grasp the entire context of just how solid your salvation and belief system is and how easily it will be too explain the concept of Jesus' completed redemption of us to God is to others. I am not telling you that everyone that you meet will be converted to your faith or your level of spiritual maturity instantly. What I do guarantee you is that you will have a firmer grasp on understanding your salvation, and when you are more confident, others will perhaps be swayed more easily by your confidence, and understanding. Through the teaching and training that you will receive in this handbook, you will be able to share your faith with renewed confidence and begin fulfilling the mandate that Jesus gave to all of us which is to go forth and make disciples.

> *And Jesus came and spoke to them, saying, "All authority has been given to Me in heaven and on earth. Go therefore and make disciples of all the nations, baptizing them in the name of the Father and of the Son and of the Holy Spirit, teaching them to observe all things that I have commanded you; and lo, I am with you always, even to the end of the age." Amen.*
>
> Matthew 28:18–20

Sharing Your Faith with an Unbeliever

Many people believe that they lack the ability or communication skills for effectively sharing their faith in God, or Jesus. This is simply a deception of the enemy of your soul, to prevent you from sharing what you know and have learned. I hope you find this book to be a tremendous help to you in sharing your faith and belief system in such a way as to lead many to Christ. If not for your own personal testimony and willingness to share, the faith of others may very well hang in balance.

Step One

People Don't Care What You Know, Until They Know That You Care

Many people believe that in order to recognize their need of a Savior, must be beat over the head with what they are doing wrong, and what they must do right. This is exactly the problem with many Christians today they think that by beating people over the head with a bible will help bring people to the saving knowledge of Christ. This is most assuredly the way to alienate people, not to gather them.

People don't want to be preached to; they want to first of all know that you care about them, and their situations in life.

Your first step in trying to share your faith effectively with anyone should be to step into their shoes (life) and find out what is important and interesting to them. You must be willing to step or I like to say, "crawl into their life," and be genuinely interested in what is of interest to them. This works with people of any age, and is particularly effective with our young people today. Many of our young people believe that we are just the old folks that don't have a clue. Young adults and teenagers need to know that we are willing to come down into their world, and find out what is important to them before they will open up and listen to what you find interesting or important. I call this tactic, Sliding God under the door into their life,(I did this with my children as they were growing up) and allowing them to see a God who is truly interested in where their interests lie. You can only perform this step if you are truly interested in what God has placed within the people that you are trying to reach for His Glory, and not your own.

Step Two

Build the relationship

We all know that in order to build a relationship, we must find some sort of common ground for the relationship to begin to grow and thrive. Building a relationship with anyone is no different from building a house, one board at a time, until it is time to be bricked and cemented together. At this point, you are sharing your life mantras, and they are sharing theirs with you as well. This is a good point to begin interjecting your belief system and values, and why you hold them so dear. With everything that they share with you about their life mantras, you can now begin to share or counter them with your life mantras, and begin to open them up to receive the next building block to your relationship, which is an understanding of your faith.

Step Three

We all need to recognize our need for God in our life

Whether you have been a Christian for a long time or for a short period, you first came to God with an understanding that you needed HIM. Regardless of whether it was a tragedy, loneliness, or just a knowing that there had to be something BIGGER than yourself, your first introduction to God was your realization that you needed HIM in your life. The following scriptures are ones that will begin to show the person that you have begun your new relationship with, that even you had to come to this realization and understanding that you needed a God who cared about you before you ever knew that HE was God, and cared for you.

> *But now the righteousness of God apart from the law is revealed, being witnessed by the Law and the Prophets, even the righteousness of God, through faith in Jesus Christ, to all and on all who believe. For there is no difference; for all have sinned and fall short of the glory of God, being justified freely by His grace through the redemption that is in Christ Jesus, who God set forth as a propitiation by His blood, through faith, to demonstrate His righteousness because in His forbearance God had passed over the sins that were previously committed, to demonstrate at the*

present time His righteousness, that He might be just and the justifier of the one who has faith in Jesus.

Romans 3:21–26

But God demonstrates His own love toward us, in that while we were still sinners, Christ died for us. Much more then, having now been justified by His blood, we shall be saved from wrath through Him. For if when we were enemies we were reconciled to God through the death of His Son, much more, having been reconciled, we shall be saved by His life. And not only that, but we also rejoice in God through our Lord Jesus Christ, through who we have now received the reconciliation.

Romans 5:8–10

Jesus answered and said to him, "Most assuredly, I say to you, unless one is born again, he cannot see the kingdom of God."

John 3:3

Through studying the scriptures just prior and just after John 3:3 we are introduced to Nicodemus who was one of the High Rulers of the Jews, and part of the most conservative groups within Israel at the time. We can compare him with what we call the conservative right wings of our times. These people, when faced with supernatural experiences will always say that God is with a person, because it fits with their understanding of God things, and they will admit that they believe that God is with a particular person. This is exactly what Nicodemus did and said to Jesus in a midnight visit with Jesus. However, Jesus had to show Nicodemus that even though he could recognize that God was with him (Jesus) and His teachings, he was only seeing from the outside in, and that in order to truly see the kingdom of God, he had to be born again. Just because we can recognize God events and happenings within our life, does not mean that we have been born again, the true born again experience will only happen upon a change of heart to accept the Son, who is Jesus.

We all have had a Nicodemus, experience in one way or another, where God has shown himself in some way. In your relationship building, you can insert your experience here and begin sharing your personal experience with God that introduced you to your need of HIM in your life. When building a relationship with people, they want to know your experiences not the experiences of someone else. One thing to remember here is that a person with only the Word of God without a testimony of God in their life will always be shown to be deficient in their Kingdom understanding. Compared to a person with The Word of God and a Testimony, who will be more complete in their Kingdom understanding, however to know and understanding is something that is *Caught NOT Taught*.

Step Four

Jesus is the Door, you are only the Knob

With all the horror movies that show a door that must be opened, our society has learned that we shouldn't open doors that look strange, act strangely, or appear hazardous to our wellbeing. With that being said, we must learn to create an inviting door of opportunity to those that we want to introduce to Jesus, not a door that seems spooky to them. (I learned this lesson the hard way with my children. I was portraying an angry God in my first few years as a born-again believer, because of the environment in which I learned of God.) We also must remember that the door that we want them to open is Jesus who is the only door by which people can come to the Father, and receive salvation. We are only the knob that opens that door.

As you are building your relationship with those who you wish to communicate your faith effectively to, you must remain real in order for people to take you and your message seriously. Only real people will describe real situations in life that we all go through, and people want to know and learn how you overcame those real problems. This was exactly the reason that I wrote my first book, "A Life of Significance" real-life stories of people who are and living Significant Lives. They don't want to hear bedtime stories and fairy tales of a better life; they want to see what a better life looks and feels like. You must allow these people into your life, to show off Jesus to them, what He has done for you in your life. In other words, you must present Jesus in such a way as to make them hungry for what you have, like a Chef that presents his plate of food in a pleasing manner. Presentation is everything.

Now when I say presentation is everything, I am not talking about how you are dressed, I am talking about how your life is dressed. This is where many Christians have gone off the track with this subject and I hope I can help to set the record straight here for all of us everyday people in everyday clothes. I had a pastor one time call my t-shirts that I wore "Cammy's anointed T-Shirts" he only said that because I refused to conform to what a member of the main prayer team should be wearing, according to someone's rules. I was always showing up in Blue Jeans, T-Shirt and Flip Flops. The way I see it is that God's seen me naked. *So why stress about the dress?* The people that we are building our relationships with don't really care if we are in a three-piece suit, or jogging shorts and a T-shirt the point of the matter is that we appear and act like real people just like they are. A prime example of this is the countless people that I have been able to minister to that didn't even know that I was a Pastor when they first got to know me. I enjoy life just as they do, laugh at funny things and have a good time and then they find out that I am a Pastor, and it freaked them out. When asked why it freaked them out to learn that I was a Pastor their response is always the same, "I would have acted differently had I known that you were a Pastor, not just a regular person." That is exactly the point that I am trying to make here, Pastors are people too, and we still put our pants on one leg at a time just like everyone else. Jesus is a real person and we are told in the scriptures that He suffered the same things just as we do and have, to show that just because He is the door to our salvation, doesn't mean that he doesn't understand our issues in life.

The following scriptures are your basic scriptures that you should be able to begin sharing within your new relationship by now. Don't be alarmed if they don't understand them when you first present them, remember, these people that you are building your relationship with are much like infants and I want you to only spoon feed them only what they can handle at this point. Just like with your baby, you put in a spoonful of food, and their tongue pushes it out, and you scrape the dribble off their chin, and spoon it back into their mouth, until they finally swallow it. This is what discipleship is all about and building relationships with unbelievers that you want to introduce to Jesus.

> *Then Jesus said to them again, "Most assuredly, I say to you, I am the door of the sheep."*
>
> John 10:7

> *Jesus said to him, "I am the way, the truth, and the life, No one come to the Father except through Me."*
>
> John 14:6

> *Nor is there salvation in any other for there is no other name under heaven given among men by which we must be saved.*
>
> Acts 4:12

As you carefully study the scriptures that are written above and look them up in your own bible, you will see that Jesus himself tells us that He is the True Shepherd, and that anyone who doesn't enter the sheepfold by the door, is a thief and a robber. Harsh words but I believe that they are effective in making us understand that Jesus is the only door into the sheepfold. Just as Jesus was explaining to Nicodemus that he was only looking at the Kingdom of God from the outside, and wasn't a true believer yet, because he hadn't entered into the sheepfold through the only door which is through HIM. You are only the doorknob that entices others to open the door into salvation, never are you the door!

Step Five

Always place your faith in Jesus and what He has done never in yourself

Christians and many church groups today place upon people the Do's and Don'ts to their faith, which are many times a turn off for most people. Society places so many rules upon us, that the last thing that we want to hear is another set of rules to live by in order to accept the free gift of salvation. Often times, the reason that people leave the established church groups for a more on non-traditional means of maintaining their faith is because of the rules that man has incorporated into the church system that Jesus NEVER introduced to us. They have completely forgotten that it is the finished work of Jesus that has provided them with their salvation not any rules that are maintained and adhered to. This is exactly what Jesus was up against is His time as a man walking and preaching His good news. *Freedom from sin is through HIS finished work, not ours.* The following scriptures are the basis for this understanding, and ones that we should take to heart throughout our walk as Christians.

> *But we are all like an unclean thing, And all our righteousness's are like filthy rags; We all fade as a leaf, And our iniquities, like the wind, Have taken us away. And there is no one who calls on Your name, Who stirs himself up to take hold of You; For You have hidden Your face from us, And have consumed us because of our iniquities. But now, O LORD, You are our Father, We are the clay, and You our potter, And all we are the work of Your hand.*
>
> Isaiah 64:6–8

For by grace you have been saved through faith, and that not of yourselves; it is the gift of God, not of works, lest anyone should boast. For we are His workmanship, created in Christ Jesus for good works which God prepared beforehand that we should walk in them.

Ephesians 2:8–10

So when Jesus had received the sour wine, He said, "It is finished!" And bowing His head, He gave up His spirit.

John 19:30

The finished work of Jesus' cross was all that was required to pay for the price that we all owed as sinners. Once He completed the payment, which was His death upon the cross, our redemption was complete and God was no longer angry with humankind. However, we must receive what Jesus did for us on that cross that day in order to become part of that Sheepfold to which he is the only door. Nothing that we can ever do will compare to the price that Jesus paid for us that day, all we can do is accept this gift, and walk in the good works that God has prepared for us to walk in once we receive Jesus as our savior. No other rules required!

Step Six

Confess, Believe and Receive!

The first question that I am always asked, "How do I accept Jesus' finished work?" The answer is quite simple, Confess Jesus as your Lord, and believe in your heart that God raised Him from the dead it just that simple. When talking one day with my son whom accepted Christ as his savior at the age of 13, he told me "well that just seems too simple." I told him "Exactly, all the work had been done now all he had to do is confess Jesus as his Lord, and believe that God raised him from the dead on the third day."

> *"The word is near you, in your mouth and in your heart" (that is, the word of faith which we preach) that if you confess with your mouth the Lord Jesus and believe in your heart that God has raised Him from the dead, you will be saved.*
>
> Romans 10:9

> *For God so loved the world that He gave His only begotten Son, that whoever believed in Him should not perish but have everlasting life. For God did not send His Son into the world to condemn the world, but that the world through Him might be saved.*
>
> John 3:16–17

Confessing Jesus as your Lord means a change in the administration over your life. Just like we receive a changing in administrations with the changing of Presidents through our elections, so do we elect Jesus as our new administration over our life. We have resigned as the lord, president and boss of our own lives, and now live through Him and his will for our life. We allow Jesus to preside on the throne of our heart instead of following our own selfish desires. Jesus creates within New Heart, a New desire, New attitude, New Life, and us way to walking out our new found salvation. Since Jesus is now the Lord of your life, you will want to make a commitment to check with Him first in all your decisions and to follow His Word and as His Spirit directs you through this NEW LIFE.

> *"Therefore whoever confesses Me before men, him I will also confess before My Father who is in heaven. But whoever denies Me before men, him I will also deny before My Father who is in heaven."*
>
> Matthew 10:32–33

Dear God in Heaven, I come to you in Jesus' name. I know that without Jesus I am lost. I don't want to be lost any longer and confess that I need Jesus as my Lord and savior. I believe with all my heart that you God have raised Jesus from the dead. I invite Jesus to reside in my heart as my savior, and invite His Spirit to take control of my life, and direct me in the good works that you have prepared for me to walk in. My old life is now gone, and the life I now live is the life that Jesus died to give me. You are now my Heavenly Father and I am now your child. Protect and guide me through the works that you have for me to do. In Jesus', mighty name, AMEN

Sharing Your Faith on Water Baptism

Water baptism is a subject that most Christians have done, but many times have not understood the true meaning or purpose of why we need to be baptized by water. The first baptism that was done in the bible was when God provided the cloud that the children of Israel walked under and the parting of the Red Sea, which allowed the children of Israel to walk across on dry ground. This baptism is called the baptism into Moses in the following scripture.

> *Moreover, brethren, I do not want you to be unaware that all our fathers were under the cloud, all passed through the sea, all were baptized into Moses in the cloud and the sea, all ate the same spiritual food, and all drank the same spiritual drink. For they drank of the spiritual Rock that followed them, and that Rock was Christ.*
>
> 1 Corinthians 10:1–4

As we continue our exploration into our understanding of water baptism, we find that the next baptism by water was performed in the days of Noah, where eight souls were saved by water, and that we learned as children about in the Old testament story of Noah building the ark and is restated for us in the following scripture.

> *Who formerly were disobedient, when once the Divine longsuffering waited in the days of Noah, while the ark was being prepared, in which a few, that is, eight souls were saved through water. There is also an antitype which now saves us—baptism (not the removal of the filth of the flesh, but the answer of a good conscience toward God), through the resurrection of Jesus Christ.*
>
> 1 Peter 3:20–21

Through the previous scripture, we see that water baptism isn't a new thing, it was a God created way for us to demonstrate our faith in God and Jesus by following in the ways that He has set for us.

Water baptism is an outward expression of our Inward confession, that Jesus is Lord!

The first reason that we are baptized by water is because we are instructed to, by Jesus in the first book of the New Testament of the bible:

> *Go therefore and make disciples of all the nations, baptizing them in the name of the Father and the Son and of the Holy Spirit.*
>
> Matthew 28:19

These words are written in red in our bible letting us know that Jesus Himself spoke these words, and everything that Jesus tells us to do is important. Now I am not saying that we shouldn't follow everything else that is said in the bible, but we should take a little more seriously Jesus' own spoken words, one of which is on being baptized. Now let's begin looking at why we need to be baptized.

> *He who believes and is baptized will be saved; but he who does not believe will be condemned.*
>
> *Mark 16:16*

If you don't believe in Jesus you won't have any desire to be baptized. Very simple and to the point I believe. Faith in Jesus only comes through speaking the word of God regarding Jesus and what He has done for us. As we begin to tell people about Jesus, they will believe or not believe, the choice is theirs to make. However, when one believes in what we are saying about our risen Lord Jesus Christ being the only begotten Son of the living God, they will desire to be baptized as the scripture states, so that their inward confession becomes an outward expression of their faith in Jesus. The following scriptures confirm this fact for us.

> *So the eunuch answered Philip and said, "I ask you, of whom does the prophet say this, of himself or of some other man?" Then Philip opened his mouth, and beginning at the Scripture; preached Jesus to him. How as they went down the road, they came to some water. And the eunuch said, "See, here is water. What hinders me from being baptized?" Then Philip said, "If you believe with all your heart, you may." And he answered and said, "I believe that Jesus Christ is the Son of God." So he commanded the chariot to stand still. And both Philip and the eunuch went down into the water, and he baptized him.*
>
> *Acts 8:34–38*

> *Then Crispus, the ruler of the synagogue, believed on the Lord with all his household. And many of the Corinthians, hearing, believed and were baptized.*
>
> *Acts 18:8*

> *What shall we say then? Shall we continue in sin that grace may abound? Certainly not! How shall we who died to sin live any longer in it? Or do you not know that as many of us as were baptized into Christ Jesus were baptized into His death? Therefore we were buried with Him through baptism into death, that just as Christ was raised from the dead by the glory of the Father, even so we also should walk in newness of life.*
>
> Romans 6:1–4

When I baptize anyone, I explain Romans 6 verses to him or her that just as I am going to dunk you fully under the water this represents your burial with Christ Jesus in His death. As I raise you up out of the water, this represents Jesus' Resurrection from the grave. As He now is the New Life, so are you now live, move, and have your being in and through HIM. When I teach children, I give them a rock to hold in their hand, and to leave it when I raise them up out of the water. The rock in their hand represents the "old man", the sinful nature before we accepted Jesus into our heart. Drop the rock as you go under the water, and when you come up you will no longer walk with that "old man" in your hand, but you are now holding the hand of Jesus NOW AND FOREVER. Through the outward expression of your baptism and you have just buried the old sinful man and now are beginning to walk in that New Life with Jesus from this point forward. You are no longer condemned and you will walk in the newness of that life that Jesus died and rose again to give you. Praise the Lord!

> *I thank you father in Jesus' name that you have allowed me to share the message and importance of water baptism with any who ask me today, and I would ask*

that you provide them with a deeper understanding than what the words that I will speak will penetrate. I only seek to do your will on this earth father, and I willing share the Gift of Jesus with everyone that I come into contact with throughout my day. In Jesus' Mighty name, AMEN.

Assurance of Salvation to All Believers

The human mind is such a magnificence and wondrous creation of God, however sometimes it can be our own worst enemy. God created our minds to hold our memories, and that is where our imagination lies as well. Often, because our minds hold both, a conflict can arise concerning our faith and belief system. The enemy of your soul uses your mind; your memories and your imagination to manipulate your thoughts, and if you don't understand the assurance of our salvation that we have received from God, then these thoughts can become tools that the enemy will try to convince you that your salvation isn't real. This is one of the most frequent "attacks" by the enemy, the devil. He will use this tactic on any believer regardless of our length of time since we were born-again.

I have two examples that I will share in story form to help demonstrate what you might come across in your travels and relationship building experiences. The first is my own personal story where as a Newly Born Again Christian; it seemed that all hell broke loose in my life after I received Christ as my Lord and Savior that night of September 18, 1988. Everyone had told me that once I received Jesus into my heart and life, I would go through what they described, as the "Honeymoon" phase to my new life, where everything would be wonderful, perfect, and nothing would go wrong for me. I am living proof, that not everyone gets the "Honeymoon" phase first. I must admit however that the first night of my salvation was wonderful, the street lights were brighter than I had ever seen them, the stars in the sky were brighter, and I seemed to have floated instead of walked to my car that night after the church service. Then the next day, there was the enemy, in full attack mode on my brain, family, EVERYTHING! The day began by a knock on the door by the sheriff's department deputies looking for my then husband, for non-payment of child support to his 1st wife. When I told him that they were looking for him, he immediately moved out of the house and moved into a commercial building that we had rented for our business. It wasn't long before our marriage began to unravel, and his lies and deceptions were exposed. I began living my life as a single mother of two children from that point however; I still had this new birth experience that wasn't very well explained to me. I didn't know that there was an enemy to my new found faith; I was simply told that I had a new life and all would be right with the world from this point forward, now that I had Jesus on my side. It would be several years actually, 10 years to be exact before I would enter into what I was told about the "Honeymoon" phase to my salvation. I wasn't taught that I could be assured of my salvation, nor was I taught anything about that there was a real enemy that hated my Jesus and my new life that I had found in Him. One afternoon, I became so angry with God that my life seemed to be a complete and utter disaster, I began screaming at Him and demanding that He show me why my life wasn't at all like what I was told or was reading about in my bible. (Special Note to the reader:

Don't try this yourself, because God WILL answers your request, and it might shock you to learn this lesson this way.) Nevertheless, how I came through this learning curve with God is the basis of this chapter how we can all be assured of our salvation regardless of the attacks that may and will come.

The second example is a story of a friend of mine, who was bedridden with ALS for several months, the disease had begun to attack her mind just prior to the Lord taking her home. You can replace the disease name with any other disease that can affect the mind and our thinking and the results will be the same. This person has begun the downward spiral into the grips of death, and the torment that the enemy can play on the feeble minded. This person was a strong and devote person of God, and the enemy attacked them at their most vulnerable moment and had convinced them that they have never been saved, and have spawned spiritual and natural children for the enemy and not of God. This can be the cruelest of attacks by the enemy but one that needs to be told, to encourage anyone that might be involved with someone in this situation. I want to let you know that yes, your loved one is still saved, they haven't lost their salvation simply because they no longer can feel like they are saved in their current feeble state, and it is actually an attack, by the enemy towards you to make you doubt your own salvation. The following scriptures will help you share your assurance of your salvation with yourself and others that you will come into contact with, and personally I believe is the biggest boost of encouragement that we can give to others in the Body of Christ.

Only you hold the key to your heart's door, and only you can allow Jesus to come into your heart as you experienced when you first believed. Just as you are the only one that can allow anyone to come into your home, and all other uninvited guests are called robbers and thieves, the same holds true to the doorway into your heart, only you hold the key to allow who come in. When you open the doorway into your heart to allow Jesus to come in, we are told by Jesus himself, after his resurrection from the grave that he stood knocking and you opened the door and allowed him to come in.

> *Behold, I stand at that the door and knock. If anyone hears My voice and opens the door, I will come in to him and dine with him, and he with Me.*
>
> Revelation 3:20

This next scripture was directly from Jesus' mouth as he was ministering to his disciples, which includes you as a disciple of Jesus Christ since you first believed in Him.

> *This is the will of the Father who sent Me, that of all He has given Me I should lose nothing, but should raise it up at that last day. And this is the will of Him who sent Me, that everyone who sees the Son and believe in Him may have everlasting life, and I will raise him up at the last day.*
>
> John 6:39 & 40

We must also remember the following scripture spoken through one of God's own Prophets in the Old Testament:

> *God is not a man, that He should lie, or a son of man, that He should repent. Has He said and will He not do? Or has He spoken, and will He not make it good?*
>
> Numbers 23:19

When you or others face a mental attack against your salvation, here are a few questions to begin to ponder and meditate on:

1. Did you open the doorway into your heart to allow Jesus to come in?
2. If you did, where is He right now?
3. Did He really come into your heart or did He lie about dining with you?

You cannot base your New Birth experience upon your fickle feelings

Your feelings are tied to your emotions, and your emotions are dependent upon many factors in your life. You can be happy, sad, angry, annoyed, overjoyed, and overwhelmed all in the course of an hour of your day. This is why you cannot and must not rely upon your feelings to give you any assurance of your salvation or new birth experience. Your assurance must come through your faith and belief system. If you have a faulty belief system or shaky faith, you will begin to doubt your salvation, and with a strong belief system and strong faith based upon God's Word, your assurance will be strong and will not waver. In the following scripture are words that Jesus himself spoke, and are often times used to manifest physical needs in our life, but I believe He was speaking on a much deeper level than that as well. I believe and have used this verse of scripture to help New and Old Christians retain their assurance in their salvation experience.

> *So Jesus answered and said to them, "Have faith in God. For assuredly, I say to you, whoever says to this*

> mountain, Be removed and be cast into the sea, and does not doubt in his heart, but believes that those things he says will be done, he will have whatever he says. Therefore I say to you, whatever things you ask when you pray, believe that you receive them, and you will have them."
>
> Mark 11:22–24

The following scriptures are used to help maintain the assurance of your New Birth Experience by reminding you that your emotions were not involved in your decision to accept Jesus in the beginning of your faith. So should neither your emotions nor your feelings be allowed to play any part in your assurance of your salvation?

> *Jesus Christ is the same yesterday, today, and forever. Do not be carried about with various and strange doctrines. For it is good that the heart be established by grace, not with foods which have not profited those who have been occupied with them.*
>
> *Hebrews 13: 8 & 9*

The scripture above speaks of not being occupied with foods, which I would like to point out here; how many times have our feelings and our emotions become our *food for thought*? So actually, we could change the word "food" in the scripture to feelings or emotions and grab a deeper understanding of our salvation.

> *Now He who has prepared us for this very thing is God, who also has given us the Spirit as a guarantee. For we walk by faith, not by sight*
>
> *II Corinthians 5:5 &7*

> *For this reason I bow my knees to the Father of our Lord Jesus Christ, from who the whole family in heaven and earth is name, that He would grant you, according to the riches of His glory, to be strengthened with might through His Spirit in the inner man, that Christ may dwell in your hearts through faith; that you being rooted and grounded in love, may be able to comprehend with all the saints what is the width and length and depth and height—to know the love of Christ which passes knowledge; that you may be filled with all the fullness of God.*
>
> Ephesians 3:14–19

Jesus NEVER changes His mind about residing in your Heart

Some people believe that once you are a born again child of God that you will never sin or do anything wrong ever again from that point. This is totally wrong thinking, however what we do have as children of God, is an advocate with the Father that has already paid the price for all of our sins, past, present and future. If you sin after you are a born again child of God, confess your sin and admit to Him (The Lord) that you were wrong and accept His forgiveness.

> *If we say that we have no sin, we deceive ourselves, and the truth is not in us. If we confess our sins, He is faithful and just to forgive us our sins and to cleanse us from all unrighteousness.*
>
> 1 John 1:8–9

> *My little children, these things I write to you, so that you may not sin. And if anyone sins, we have an Advocate with the Father, Jesus Christ the righteous. And He*

> Himself is the propitiation for our sins, and not for ours only but also for the whole world.
>
> 1 John 2:1 & 2

When we knowingly or unknowingly commit a sin or wrong behavior within our daily walk as a child of God, the Spirit will prick our hearts' to let us know that there is something wrong with our fellowship with Him. It's not that He leaves us; it is a fact that just like we do our natural children when they have committed a wrong action or behavior we correct them, so too will the Lord correct us as His children.

> "My son, do not despise the chastening of the LORD, Nor be discouraged when you are rebuked by Him; For whom the LORD loves He chastens, And scourges every son who He receives." If you endure chastening, God deals with you as with sons; for what son is there whom a father does not chasten?
>
> Hebrews 12:5–7

He will never leave you

Contrary to some who say differently, the Lord will NEVER leave you or forsake you. You are His child and nothing or no one can take you out of His hand. Once you have made the decision to accept Jesus as your Lord and Savior, it is a FINISHED and COMPLETED deal. Jesus doesn't take back His Spirit, and never again will you be without Him in your life. Always remember, that at times during your life, you will see two sets of footprints along the sandy shores, and you know that He is walking along side of you. At other times in your life, you will only see one set of footprints in the sandy shores, and this is when you know that He is carrying you in His arms through your situation.

> *Let your conduct be without covetousness; be content with such things as you have. Foe He Himself has said, "I will never leave you nor forsake you."*
>
> *Hebrews 13:5 & 6*

> *"All authority has been given to Me in heaven and on earth. Go therefore and make disciples of all the nations, baptizing them in the name of the Father and of the Son and of the Holy Spirit, teaching them to observe all things that I have commanded you; and lo, I am with you always, even to the end of the age." Amen.*
>
> *Dear Heavenly Father, you have given me the assurance that I needed to have, and now understand that my salvation is a forever salvation given to me as a free gift through the finished work of your dear Son, Jesus Christ. I accept this assurance based upon your Word, and that you are Not a Man that you should lie, but that every Word that you have spoken resides within my heart to know that I am your child, a Child of the Most High God, never to be forsaken. AMEN!*
>
> *Matthew 28:18–20*

Baptism of the Holy Spirit

One of the most controversial subjects within the Christian community is the topic of the baptism of the Holy Spirit. I believe that the reason for this controversy is that the enemy, the devil, knows that when we receive the special gift that God has provided for each of His children, he, the devil, becomes debilitate in his efforts to manipulate us into unbelief. As we explore this subject, I believe the scriptures will reveal to each of you, the readers, a new understanding and enlightenment to understand our need, especially in today's time, the need for such a special gift from our Heavenly Father.

The first issue that needs to be addressed before we begin exploring the scriptural basis of being baptized with the Holy Spirit is the misinformation that has been spread regarding this subject. The baptism of the Holy Spirit is NOT REQUIRED in order to be saved, it is a Gift from your Heavenly Father God and you have the choice to receive it or not as His Child. The only requirement for receiving this free gift is that first you must be a born again child of God before you can receive this Gift. Just like you have the choice to receive a package that comes in the mail to you that you must sign for, you have the option to refuse the package and it is simply returned to the sender. The same holds true for the Baptism of the Holy Spirit, you are not required to receive it, and it is an optional FREE GIFT to all born again children of God.

The second issue surrounding the Baptism of the Holy Spirit is that, YES when you receive this optional FREE GIFT from God, you will only speak in other tongues as the Spirit gives the utterance if you allow the Spirit of God to speak through you. Notice that I said if you allow the Spirit of God to speak through you. This is correct, your part in receiving your new language is yielding your tongue to what the Spirit of God wants spoken. No yielding of your tongue means that no Heavenly Language will be spoken forth. This gift of "Other tongues" or "heavenly language" is NOT and I repeat NOT taught by man, it is caught through the Spirit of God. Let no man deceive you in this, the new language that comes as proof or evidence that you have received the Baptism of the Holy Spirit cannot be taught to you from another person, it is the Spirit of God putting His language within you and you speaking forth what He wants spoken. Just as you had to learn language skills from the time, you began growing up as a natural child of your natural parents, the same holds true with the new Heavenly Language skills. Your skill and proficiency of speaking in your new language will be developed over the course of your lifetime.

A word of caution before we begin exploring the scriptures regarding the Baptism of the Holy Spirit. This Gift is only available to born again children of God. The reason for this is; *if you ask for this gift prior to becoming a born again child of God by asking Jesus into your heart first, what you will end up with is a spiritual empowerment from the enemy, the devil.* You must realize and understand that there is a very real enemy called the devil, who doesn't want you to banish him and his demonic stronghold over your life. By becoming a born again child of God, you have banished his demonic stronghold on your life. Therefore, if you were to ask for the baptism of the Holy Spirit prior to becoming a child of God, you are opening yourself up to a demonic force to come in and mimic what God wants His children to have. The devil has no real power, he only has the power to copy what God has already created, and this is why you must receive Jesus as your Lord and Savior prior to asking for the Baptism of the Holy Spirit.

The Baptism of the Holy Spirit is NOT a new thing it was spoken of by the Old Testament Prophet Ezekiel

This highly controversial subject is not a new happening in the modern day church, God had His Prophet Ezekiel begin speaking about this subject long before Jesus ever walked the earth.

> *I will give you a new heart and put a new spirit within you; I will take the heart of stone out of your flesh and give you a heart of flesh. I will put My Spirit within you and cause you to walk in My statutes, and you will keep My judgments and do them.*
>
> *Ezekiel 36:26 & 27*

The Lord, speaking through Ezekiel is talking with the children of Israel at this particular moment in time, however, it is also applicable to the world, who does not know or have Jesus in their hearts yet. When God speaks, he will often tell us what he is going to do prior to actually doing it, much in the same way that teachers will tell you when to expect an exam, or when a field trip is going to take place. Notice, as you study this scripture out in your own bible that God wasn't saying that NOW they have that new spirit, and new heart of flesh, but one day they WILL have it. Again, in the following scripture we see that God had spoken through another prophet this time in the new testament of the bible, through John the Baptist, who proclaimed that the one that would baptize us with the Holy Spirit had finally arrived.

> *And John bore witness, saying, "I saw the Spirit descending from heaven like a dove, and He remained upon Him. I did not know Him, but He who sent me to baptize with water said to me, 'Upon whom you see the Spirit descending, and remaining on Him, this is He who baptizes with the Holy Spirit.' And I have seen and testified that this is the Son of God."*
>
> John 1:32–34

The world, those without Christ cannot receive the Baptism of the Holy Spirit

Jesus himself spoke of the Holy Spirit to his disciples in the following scripture, however He referred to Him as a helper, which when we study it out, is another word for the Spirit of God comes to reside within us. Jesus also said that the Holy Spirit was only for those you had received and loved Him, and because the world hasn't received and loved Him they could not see the Holy Spirit, or receive Him.

> *"If you love Me, keep My commandments. And I will pray the Father, and He will give you another Helper, that He*

may abide with you forever—the Spirit of truth, whom the world cannot receive, because it neither sees Him nor knows Him; but you know Him, for He dwells with you and will be in you. I will not leave you orphans; I will come to you."

John 14:15–18

Once ANYONE receives Jesus then they become eligible to receive the Baptism of the Holy Spirit

For God so loved the world that He gave His only begotten Son, that whoever believes in Him should not perish but have everlasting life. For God did not send His Son into the world to condemn the world, but that the world through Him might be saved.

John 3:16–17

The Holy Spirit is only for God's children

In the following scriptures, the Holy Spirit was only given to those that followed the instructions given by the Risen Christ. At this point, the disciples didn't know what to ask for, and Jesus was instructing them to stay in their assigned place until the promise came. Now I am sure, that if you and I had been living during this time, we to would have forgotten all about the words that He and John the Baptist had spoken about this Holy Spirit. This is why I believe that we are allowed to ask and the disciples just had to wait, because if you don't know what to ask for, how can you ask to receive it?

> *And being assembled together with them, He commanded them not to depart from Jerusalem, but to wait for the Promise of the Father, "which," He said, "you have heard from Me, for John truly baptized with water, but you shall be baptized with the Holy Spirit not many days from now."*
>
> Acts 1:4–5

> *Then Peter said to them, "Repent, and let every one of you be baptized in the name of Jesus Christ for the remission of sins; and you shall receive the gift of the Holy Spirit. For the promise is to you and to your children, and to all who are afar off, as many as the Lord our God will call."*
>
> Acts 2:38–39

If you don't unwrap all of the Gifts you haven't received them yet

Just believing in Jesus as your savior, does not mean that you have received the Baptism of the Holy Spirit that He and the Father have promised. In the following scripture, Paul after having been baptized with the Holy Spirit, came to a church that was baptizing people that believed in Jesus, however they hadn't receive or even heard of the Holy Spirit at this point. This is also true with many of our denominational and nondenominational churches today as well. Many do not teach anything about the Holy Spirit, they only teach about the remission of our sins, and the baptism with water that signifies that our sins have been washed away. Please don't misunderstand me, water baptism is still a very important part in the process, but it is NOT the final part of the WHOLE unwrapped gift that

God was giving us. It is much like a box within a box type of gift. Once you unwrap the outer package that you are receiving, the best is yet to come with the inner wrapped package. There are a great many number of Christians who have only unwrapped the outer gift, and didn't know that there was another more powerful gift just waiting to be unwrapped and received.

> *And it happened, while Apollos was at Corinth, that Paul, having passed through the upper regions, came to Ephesus. And finding some disciples he said to them, "Did you receive the Holy Spirit when you believed?" So they said to him, "We have not so much as heard whether there is a Holy Spirit." And he said to them, "Into what then were you baptized?' So they said, "Into John's baptism." Then Paul said, "John indeed baptized with a baptism of repentance, saying to the people that they should believe on Him who would come after him, that is, on Christ Jesus." When they hear this, they were baptized in the name of the Lord Jesus. And when Paul had laid hand on them, the Holy Spirit came upon them, and they spoke with tongues and prophesied.*
>
> Acts 19:1–6

Once you are a Child of God there is NOTHING to fear about asking and receiving the Baptism of the Holy Spirit.

As I cautioned you earlier in this chapter, about not asking for this Gift without being a child of God first. Those that are His children have NOTHING to fear in asking to receive this freely given gift. Just like with your own children who come to you and ask for something, do you trick them into asking for something good, and then give them something that would harm them? I should think NOT. And so is true with our Heavenly Father, neither will He give you something that would harm you. He is a much better Father than we are. So have NO FEAR child of God, ask and you shall receive.

> *"For everyone who asks receives, and he who seeks finds, and to him who knocks it will be opened. If a son asks for bread from any father among you, will he give him a stone? Or if he asks for a fish, will he give him a serpent instead of a fish? Of if he asks for an egg, will he offer him a scorpion? If you then, being evil, know how to give good gifts to your children, how much more will your heavenly Father give the Holy Spirit to those who ask Him!"*
>
> Luke 11:10–13

The Purpose of the Holy Spirit is POWER

Have you ever noticed that some preachers and teachers of the Word of God can captivate a group of people with the Word that they speak, while others seem to be very dry and boring? The reason for this is one has the Holy Spirit and one does not. One teacher or preacher is giving you the word without having the power of the Holy Spirit within his words. The other teacher/preacher gives you the Word with the Power of the Holy Spirit, which brings life into his words. This Holy Spirit Power from on high makes all the difference in the delivery and receiving of the spoken word. This same captivating Power is available to every child of God through the gift of the Holy Spirit.

And we have such trust through Christ toward God. Not that we are sufficient of ourselves to think of anything as being from ourselves, but our sufficiency is from God, who also made us sufficient as ministers of the new covenant, not of the letter but of the Spirit; for the letter kills, but the Spirit gives life.

2 Corinthians 3:4–6

"But you shall receive power when the Holy Spirit has come upon you; and you shall be witnesses to Me in Jerusalem, and in all Judea and Samaria, and to the end of the earth."

Acts 1:8

Additional Benefits from unwrapping the Gift of the Holy Spirit

Power is the predominate benefit to receiving the baptism of the Holy Spirit, however there are many other benefits to unwrapping this most precious gift from your Heavenly Father as well. Have you ever had those times in your life where you just didn't know how to pray for a particular situation? Or a day, that you just were feeling humdrum and just couldn't seem to get the motivation to carry out your normal routine for the day? The answer is of course you have, we all have, and this is normal for all humans living on planet earth today. However, God in His marvelous way has provided an answer for just such times. The baptism of the Holy Spirit revives and rejuvenates our human spirit. Basically, the Holy Spirit wakes us up and is the extra boost that we sometimes need to get through our day. Furthermore, by praying in your Most Holy Faith language of the Holy Spirit He will tell you of things to come, so that you will be properly armed for whatever comes your way in life. A prime example of this benefit of being Baptized with the Holy Spirit is shown in the following story.

Around 6:30 am one morning, I was sitting minding my own business, not really thinking about much of anything except drinking my coffee. Suddenly, the Holy Spirit begins having me pray in my heavenly language, and from the intensity and urgency that seemed to be resounding in my prayer language, I knew that the Holy Spirit was having me pray for something very important. Just as suddenly as my prayer language had started, in about 2 or 3 minutes I was through praying. I asked the Father, "What was that all about?" Immediately I received an answer, "Marcus has been in a wreck." I didn't get upset, I didn't cry, I really didn't have any emotion at all. I stood up and walked into my bedroom to get something, and suddenly the phone rings and it is Marcus telling me, "Mom, I have been in a wreck, can you come get me because the truck won't make it home." At this point, I don't know whether to cry, because my son was just in a wreck, or to Praise the Lord, because He had told me of things to come, and had me praying over a situation that I didn't even know that was happening at the time.

I arrived at the accident site about the same time that the police had arrived, and was shocked to see my son, standing beside his truck, that had obviously been in a rollover wreck, and was in the ditch on the side of the road. After talking with the police and witnesses to the accident, we determined that at the exact time that the Holy Spirit began having me pray in my heavenly language, Marcus was about to be broadsided by an 18-wheeler truck. He had fallen asleep, and was swerving into the oncoming lane of traffic, Marcus woke up and tried to correct the swerve and began rolling in his truck. Witnesses told me that they saw the truck roll about 2-1/2 times before it came to a stop in the ditch. Each of the witnesses said that they didn't know how or why the 18-wheeler didn't hit him, it was a true miracle. Marcus didn't have injuries, except maybe his pride that day. The interesting thing about Marcus not having any injuries from the wreck was that he had a head full of dirt, and the back of his left shoulder of his white shirt had dirt streaks embedded into the fabric. When I asked him how all the dirt got on his shirt like that, and in his hair, he said, "Mom, all I know is that the upper half of my body was kind of hanging out the window as I was sliding to a stop over there in the ditch." Look at what the Lord has done! He protected my son and had me praying over a situation that I had no idea was happening at the time. All because I willing received and unwrapped the gift of the Holy Spirit all those years ago, God had me praying protection over my youngest son the week before his 21st birthday. Praise the Lord!

> *However, when He, the Spirit of truth, has come, He will guide you into all truth; for He will not speak on His own authority, but whatever He hears He will speak; and He will tell you things to come.*
>
> John 16:13

> *For he who speaks in a tongue does not speak to men but to God, for no one understand him; however, in the spirit he speaks mysteries.*
>
> 1 Corinthians 14:2

He who speaks in a tongue edifies himself, but he who prophesies edifies the church.

1 Corinthians 14:4

Likewise the Spirit also helps in our weaknesses. For we do not know what we should pray for as we ought, but the Spirit Himself makes intercession for us with groanings which cannot be utter. Now He who searches the hearts knows what the mind of the Spirit is, because He makes intercession for the saints according to the will of God.

Romans 8:26 & 27

But you, beloved, building yourselves up on your most holy faith, praying in the Holy Spirit, keep yourselves in the love of God, looking for the mercy of our Lord Jesus Christ unto eternal life.

Jude 20 & 21

Evidence that you have unwrapped the inner gift inside your gift of Salvation

Every gift that you receive in the natural is seen, just as every gift given by God can be seen by the evidence that it has been received. Just as every birthday that comes around you must open your presents in order to effectively receive that gift, right? Once you open the gift, everyone including you can see what you have received, correct? The same hold true for the Gifts that God gives us. The evidence that we have received the Holy Spirit as God had promised to give us when we ask is that we will begin to speak with a language not previously known to us. This is what is called tongues or some call our Heavenly Language. It is a language, with verbs, and nouns, etc… you just have never been taught this language it is free evidence that you have unwrapped that inner gift inside the gift of your salvation. Through the following scriptures we should have nailed the facts down that if you have ask for and received the Baptism of the Holy Spirit, there will be evidence of you having received that gift.

> *And they were all filled with the Holy Spirit and began to speak with other tongues, as the Spirit gave them utterance.*
>
> Acts 2:4

> *While Peter was still speaking these words, the Holy Spirit fell upon all those who heard the word. And those of the circumcision who believed were astonished, as many as came with Peter, because the gift of the Holy Spirit had been poured out on the Gentiles also, For they hears them speak with tongues and magnify God.*
>
> Acts 10:44–46

> *Dear Heavenly Father, I come to you in the name of Jesus. You told me in your word that if I as your child ask you for the gift of the Holy Spirit you would gladly give me that gift. You also said in your word that when I have received the Holy Spirit, that I will receive power to be a witness for Jesus. I know that I am your child, Father, and I am born of your Spirit, washed in the blood of Jesus and I thank you for that. I need more power in my life Father, the power that only comes from the Holy Spirit dwelling within me. I desire to be a greater witness for Jesus on this earth. I ask you now for the gift of the Holy Spirit. Fill me with your Spirit right now Lord Jesus. I receive that free gift now, and*

by faith I will begin to speak with other tongues, not in a language that is known to me, but in that Heavenly language that I have learned about that is available only to your children. In Jesus' mighty name, AMEN!

If you have prayed and asked the Father to receive the Holy Spirit, begin to speak whatever sounds or syllables that comes to you. I have heard people tell me that they "hear" deep within them a voice and others tell me that they see a "ticker tape" type thing in their minds eye. Either way, you will not understand it with your natural mind, and just like a baby first learning to talk, you will be beginning to speak a new language, and it will be developed and matured with time. Have faith and believe that you have received the Holy Spirit, and I encourage you to begin to pray daily in your new heavenly language and with practice, your new language will be fully developed and will allow you to grow in the Spirit with exponential growth from the power that you now have been given.

One other piece of advice that my editor reminded me of about this topic is that when you ask to receive the Baptisim of the Holy Spirit, what happened to her was that she began hearing a foreign language coming up for deep inside herself, as well as a tremendous warmth cover her entire body. She had to yield her tongue and begin speaking out the language that she heard and felt coming up for deep within her.

He that believeth in Me, as the Scripture hath said, out of his belly shall flow rivers of living water."

John 7:38

Healing to the Sick

This may be the first time that you are learning about healing, or you may have heard about healing but thought it as being too mysterious so you left it alone. Regardless of what camp you are in on this subject, through this chapter I will show you that it is the Lord's will that all are healed, however, not all have their faith developed for healing. Through the scriptures and testimonies that you will read, you will learn that healing is available to all who will believe and receive.

I was first introduced to the Healing Power of God through my first church congregation that I was a member of. Several people within the congregation had testimonies of how the Lord had healed them, and one testimony in particular has stuck with me for the past 25 years. This woman had been diagnosed with stage IV lung cancer, and has shared her testimony of how the Lord healed her, and she has remained alive for the past 25 years and counting. I didn't gain my knowledge and understanding about the healing power of God though until the last 10 years, when I was privileged to begin working with another Pastor that expanded my understanding on the many facets of the Word of God, especially in gaining a greater understanding of God's healing power.

Though working with this Pastor/Mentor of mine, I saw countless people healed and made whole through the miracle working power of God, and assisted him on writing a couple of his books during my tenure with him. It was after his last book *Your Healing Door* that God released me to begin my own ministry, and started me on the journey to begin teaching and writing books to help other, Christians develop their faith. One of the key areas that the Lord has had me teach on is this area of healing, and helping people just like I was in the beginning to learn and understand that healing is for everyone, not just a select few. Through the scriptures that I will provide and the testimonies that I will share, you will begin to become enlightened on this often times misunderstood benefit in God's miracle working power.

The first story or testimony of God's healing power that I would like to share with you is one of a dear friend of mine. She was in her words, "Baptized a Catholic, but now is a Born-Again Child of God." Nancy was one of those dyed in the wool Catholics that still prayed the rosary, and saw Jesus still hanging on the Cross of her crucifix. However, she was also one of the children in her Catholic school days that were always getting into trouble for asking too many questions and the Nuns couldn't or wouldn't answer. God introduced us to each other about 25 years ago, and let me tell you, that had to have had God laughing at our comedic friendship. Here I was a Pentecostal Christian and there she was a dyed in the wool Catholic, and through the first several years we never discussed religion or faith or anything that might have derailed our friendship. It was only after we had been friends for about 3 years that we began having any type of spiritual conversations. I know that I carried a bruise in the middle of my forehead for the next year or so because I felt like I was banging my head up against a brick wall while her faith was being developed. However, what she needed to learn is to get to the other side or backside of the cross, to his resurrection power that is available to all. Catholics have an excellent understanding on the spiritual aspects to our faith in Jesus; however, they sometimes are often a little misguided about the object of their faith however. They completely believe in Jesus, but also believe that they must pray to Jesus' mother in order to get their prayers answered or heard. This is the area that Nancy and I had to deal with first. Let me state for the record, whenever I am dealing with Catholics, I share with them scriptures and tell them to read it in their own bible. Hint: NEVER tell a Catholic not to read their own bible, unless you want a real fight, and one fight that you will never win. They must read the scriptures in their own Catholic bible before they will ever believe what you have to say regarding the scriptures.

As the years past, and our relationship developed, and my learning increased in respect to God's healing power, I began sharing with her about some meetings that I was attending where the Power of God was there and healing a great number of people whom I personally knew. I shared with her the testimony of how my youngest son had gone with me to one of the meetings, and was healed from a severe case of warts that seemed to cover both of his hands. Through me sharing this and many other testimonies, and little did I know, she herself was suffering from an ailment that was causing her some concern, her faith was increased to the point that she believed what I was telling her, and she acted on that faith and was healed.

Nancy for several weeks had a lump on her leg that was causing her great concern. Her dad had died of a blood clot, and what she saw on her leg looked to be a blood clot that was the source of her concern. As I was telling her about all the healing miracles that were taking place at the meetings that I was attending, and our relationship had already developed the attitude and understanding that I wasn't guiding her astray on the Word of God. Her faith began being increased to the point that she believed that she too could be healed by her faith in God's healing power. One morning after one of the meetings that I was telling her about, she decided that she believed what I was telling her, and so she began to pray about the lump on her leg, and she told me later that she heard the Lord tell her, "push on it". She also told me that when she heard this her mind began screaming, "if you push on it, it will move up to your brain, and you will die." And after the many hours of my teaching her not to listen to what your brain screams only listen to what you believe the Lord is saying, she pressed on the lump, and within a few moments, the lump was gone, and she was completely healed of this stress causing lump. She called me up and told me what had happened and we rejoiced together over what the Lord had done through just me sharing healing testimonies.

Notice that through Nancy's testimony of her healing, there was nothing "spooky spiritual" about it. Only that she believed and received her healing. Notice also, that it was through our relationship that had been built up over several years and based on trusting me not to lie or lead her astray that allowed her faith to be built up enough to believe and receive her healing. This is the main KEY, to building up your faith or anyone else's faith. The Kingdom of God is built upon Revelation and Relationship. Revelation of God's Word, and building upon the relationship with

God and others are the pillars that God's Kingdom stands and walk on in this earth. If you don't build relationships with others, then you aren't building upon your Revelation knowledge of God and his Word.

Throughout the Word of God, there are numerous scriptures regarding walking in Divine health and healing. There is no formula or magic spell when healing is received it is only received by faith in the Word and Works of God, period. When you try to prescribe a formula for sharing the healing Power of God, is when the enemy has gotten you to think that you have to work for your healing somehow and has deceived you. There is NO WORK involved in God's healing; only having faith to receive it. If you are ministering healing to a friend or family member, you must have developed a relationship with that friend or family member first, before their faith will be built up enough to believe and receive the Word of God that you are sharing with them. Another Key to assisting people with building up their faith is that; you can't win anyone to the Lord, whom you first haven't won to yourself. If people can trust you, then they can trust God and His miracle working power that you are sharing with them.

The key that will unlock healing for the people that you are around is the relationships that you have built with them as you are building your own faith in the Word of God for healing. God's mighty power will begin to flow and to be shared throughout your sphere of influence to those around and that are connected to you, as your relationship with God and others is developed. Your faith will be developed through your faith of standing on His Word for any healing situations that are needed in your life or those around you.

The main scriptures that all the healing hangs on are supported by, Isaiah 53:5 regarding what Jesus did for all of us that day as He received the punishment that we all deserved:

> *But He was wounded for our transgressions, He was bruised for our iniquities; The chastisement for our peace was upon Him, And by His stripes we are healed.*
>
> Isaiah 53:5

> *His mother said to the servants, "Whatever He says to you, do it."*
>
> John 2:5

> *Looking unto Jesus, the author and finisher of our faith, who for the joy that was set before Him endured the cross, despising the shame, and has sat down at the right hand of the throne of God.*
>
> Hebrews 12:2

You first must have a true faith and belief that Jesus died, rose, and is seated at the Right hand of the Father before you can ever begin to have faith in the Healing Power of God.

Jesus only came to do three things To Preach, To Teach and To Heal. Jesus preached the good news of the Gospel everywhere He went, and taught that faith not sacrifice was what God required, and He healed all that were oppressed by the devil. If we want to do what Jesus did, then these are the three things that every believer should be doing throughout their lifetime. To preach something is a fancy way to say expound on a topic. You don't have to have a pulpit to preach what you know and believe, you only have to have your faith, and God will begin to open up your understanding to enable you to expound on that topic so that others can come to your same level of understanding and faith regarding the subject. Jesus spoke to people one on one, and He preached to the multitudes. The same holds true for you and me. We can expound on our faith and understanding to a group or can expound one-on-one. It makes no difference. As you teach others, their faith along with your own will begin to be developed for whatever situation that may arise. No magic, no spooky spiritual concoctions, just your faith and willingness to share with others will bring healing to the nations. Believe, Receive and Share!

I would like to place a side note to this chapter on the gift of healing. Just as you didn't know everything connected to the car before you began driving at 16 years old. Neither do any of us completely understand why when we pray for some folks and they receive their healing immediately and others seem to take a bit longer to receive and sometimes go on to heaven without their healing manifested here on earth. We aren't required to know everything, only to be a vessel for God to move and have his way in this earth. Maybe all won't be healed but I guarantee you that your faith and obedience to God will provide comfort and sometimes that extra big hammer is required for those special situations that require multiple peoples prayer of faith and believing. A prime example of this was an interview I did while helping a pastor write his books, and an older woman who had been told by her doctor, that she had a mass in her stomach. This woman was a strong woman of Faith in our church. She prayed after receiving that not so good report, and heard the Lord tell her that she needed to call the elders of the church together and pray that she was healed. The following week, she went back to the same doctor and when they did the sonogram for another check of her stomach before deciding their next step, the mass was GONE! Praise the Lord! She believed, and received her healing.

Your Active Believing Faith Without Doubting.

And Jesus went about all Galilee, teaching in their synagogues, preaching the gospel of the kingdom, and healing all kinds of sickness and all kinds of disease among the people. Then His face went throughout all Syria; and they brought to Him all sick people who were afflicted with various diseases and torments, and those who were demon-possessed, epileptics, and paralytics; and He healed them. Great multitudes followed Him—from Galilee, and from Decapolis, Jerusalem, Judea, and beyond the Jordon.

Matthew 4:23–25

Then He called His twelve disciples together and gave them power and authority over all demons, and to cure diseases. He sent them to preach the kingdom of God and to heal the sick. And He said to them, "Take nothing for the journey, neither staffs, nor bag nor bread not money; and do not have two tunics apiece. "Whatever house you enter, stay there, and from there depart. And whoever will not receive you; when you go out of that city, shake off the very dust from your feet as a testimony against them." So they departed and went through the towns, preaching the gospel and healing everywhere.

Luke 9:1–6

"I do not pray for these alone, but also for those who will believe in Me through their word; that they will may be one, as You, Father, are in Me, and I in You that they also may be one in Us, that the world may believe that You sent Me. And the glory with You gave Me I have given them, that they may be one just as We are one: I in them and You in Me; that they may be made perfect in one, and that the world may know that You have sent Me, and have loved them as You have loved Me. Father, I desire that they also whom You gave Me may be with Me where I am, that they may behold My glory which You have given Me; for You loved Me before the foundation of the world. O righteous Father! The world has not known You, but I have known You; and these have known that You sent Me. And I have declared to them Your name, and will declare it, that the love with which You loved Me may be in them, and I in them."

John 17:20–26

Dear Heavenly Father, I now understand that through your Son, Jesus Christ, that I have the same healing power residing within me that Jesus has, and I pray that you guide the sick across my path today and every day, to share your healing power with them. In Jesus' Mighty Name, AMEN!

Prayer — Talking to Your Father

If there is one topic in the Christian Faith that causes people's eyes to glaze over, and have that "deer in the headlights" look, it is this subject. Actually, I was one of those in the beginning. When I first began my relationship with Jesus, prayer of one of those things that only the ultra-religious people did, and I didn't understand it. The Pastor would call for an "official" prayer meeting and the only people that would attend would be those people that I felt that I would never attain. Don't get me wrong, I believed that Jesus was with me, and that he would never leave me, but how this prayer thing worked was a mystery to me. Even Jesus' disciples had the same questions and "deer in the headlights" looks when they asked Jesus how to pray. Allow me to take the mystery, intrigue, and wonderment out of this once and for all through this chapter.

Prayer is simply having a conversation. Reminding God of His Word that you are standing on for your specific need.

Another thing about prayer that confused me when I was a "Newly Born-again Christian" was that when Jesus talked with His disciples about prayer in Matthew chapter 6 what everyone calls "The Lord's Prayer" really is only an outline on how to pray.

> *In this manner, therefore, pray:*
> *Our Father in heaven,*
> *Hallowed by Your name.*
> *Your Kingdom come.*
> *Your will be done*
> *On earth as it is in heave.*
> *Give us this day our daily bread.*
> *And forgive us our debts,*
> *As we forgive our debtors.*
> *And do not lead us into temptation,*
> *But deliver us from the evil one.*
> *For Yours is the kingdom and the power and the glory forever. Amen*
>
> Matthew 6:9–13

Part one of Prayer according to Jesus' instructions is to acknowledge God as YOUR Father, not someone whom you don't know, but YOUR FATHER. It's all about identity, your identity in Christ allows you access to God because He IS your Father if you have accepted his only begotten Son, Jesus.

Part Two, of prayer according to Jesus, is calling forth the Kingdom of God in and through your life as a Child of God. In God's Kingdom, His Word is his covenant agreement with each of his children. As children of God, our first assignment is to infiltrate this "world" with His Kingdom light.

Part Three, is give us our daily bread. The daily bread that Jesus speaks of is the bread of life which is The Word of God. Whatever your need for the day, you should have a scripture to begin reminding God and yourself of. Each verse of scripture is a full five course meal if we only feed on what He has said and state it back to Him. Not that he doesn't remember His word, but it's to let you know, that you know, what He has said in His Word. If you don't know scripture, find it and begin feeding on it.

Part Four, is forgiveness. Forgiving others trespasses against us is probably the one thing that prevents so many Christians from seeing and receiving answers to their prayers. If you are trying to stand on a verse of scripture over your life and hold any unforgiveness or bitterness in your heart towards another, your answers to your prayer will be hindered. As a disciple of Christ, you are held to a higher standard because you should know that you are to walk in forgiveness toward others so that your Father in Heaven will hear and answer your prayers. This is why when New Christians pray, it seems that they get answers to their prayers more rapidly than Christians that have been in the faith for a while, they are older in the faith and should know that forgiveness of others is a primary key to answered prayers. Forgiveness IS NOT letting someone else off the hook, but in fact it gets you off the hook when you forgive. Matthew chapter 18:21–35 spells this out perfectly.

> *The Peter came to Him and said, "Lord, how often shall my brother sin against me, and I forgive him? Up to seven times?*
>
> *Jesus said to him, "I do not say to you, up to seven times, but up to seventy times seven. Therefore the kingdom of heaven is like a certain king who wanted to settle accounts with his servants. And when he had begun to settle accounts, one was brought to him who owed him ten thousand talents. But as he was not able to pay, his master commanded that he be sold, with his*

wife and children and all that he had, and that payment be made. The servant therefore fell down before him, saying, 'Master, have patience with me, and I will pay you all.' The the master of that servant was moved with compassion, released him, and forgave him the debt.

But that servant went out and found one of his fellow servants who owed him a hundred denarii; and he laid hands on him and took him by the throat, saying 'Pay me what you owe! Sohis fellow servant fell down at his feet and begged him, saying 'Have patience with me, and I will pay you all. And he would not, but went and threw him into prison till he should pay the debt. So when his fellow servants saw what had been done, they were very grieved, and came and told their master all that had been done. Then his master, after he had called him, said to him, 'You wicked servant! I forgave you all that debt because you begged me. Should you not also have had compassion on your fellow servant, just as I had pity on you? And his master was angry, and delivered him to the torturers until he should pay all that was due to him.

"*So My heavenly Father also will do to you if each of you, from his heart, does not forgive his brother his trespasses.*"

Matthew 18:21–35

I cannot tell you how many people I counsel with that seem to be frustrated because they aren't seeing the answers to their prayers as they thought they should. And 9 out of 10 times when we get to the root of the issue, there is unforgiveness at the root. As these same people tell their testimony of healing, major blessings, family reconciliations etc… somewhere in each of their testimonies of standing on God's Word for a specific reason, always has an area in their own life that needs attention before their prayers were answered. God's not going to beat you over the head for any unforgiveness that you might hold in your heart, but it has been my experience that He will gently and loving answer your prayer through guiding you through a growth period, to allow you to see for yourself where the hindrances to your prayers lies. Once the hindrances are removed... your answer was all the time waiting right there for you to receive. God is a lot like the way we are with raising our children. Just because our children ask for a specific "thing" doesn't mean that they are ready to handle it. God has the absolute BEST in mind for you, Spirit, Soul and Body, so to get you there He will loving guide you through the conversation and lessons that you need to learn through forgiving others if you allow Him.

> *"For if you forgive men, their trespasses, your heavenly Father will also forgive you. But if you do not forgive men their trespasses, neither will your Father forgive your trespasses.*
>
> Matthew 6:14

The other thing that I have seen hinder our prayers is UNBELIEF. It is actually an identity crisis that we are having because we don't actually believe that we are IN HIM, after we have believed. However, even Jesus himself was dealing with unbelief issue with his disciples and others. the father of the boy recognized that he didn't believe fully as we can see in the conversation between the boy's father and Jesus in:

> *Jesus said to him, "If you can believe," all things are possible to him who believes."*

> *Immediately the father of the child cried out and said with tears, "Lord, I believe; help my unbelief!"*
>
> Mark 9:23–24

Your heavenly Father already knows whether you believe or not. The point of the matter is that if we are faithful in confessing our unbelief to Him, He will answer our prayer just as Jesus did that day for the father's son in the above conversation with Jesus.

If we are to ever get past this identity crisis that we often have we need to see John chapter 17 as the true Lord's prayer for each of us, and this prayer is a prayer not an outline on how to pray. Notice that Jesus continually reminds the Father of His Word, and you can also see the steps that we discussed earlier on how to pray.

The Actual Lord's Prayer

"I do not pray for these alone, but also for those who will believe in Me through their word; that they all may be one, as You, Father, are in Me, and I in You; that they also may be one in Us, that the world may believe that You sent Me. And the glory which You gave Me I have given them, that they may be one just as We are one: I in them, and You in Me; that they may be made perfect in one, and that the world may know that You have love Me.

"After, I desire that they also whom You gave Me may be with Me where I am, that they may behold My glory which You have given Me; for You love Me before the foundation of the world. O righteous Father! The world has not known You, but I have known You; and these have known that You sent Me. And I have declared to them Your name, and will declare it, that

> *the love with which You loved Me may be in them, and I in them."*
>
> *John 17:20–26*

So it comes down to this; If you aren't seeing answers to your prayers, first check your own heart to see if there is any unforgiveness that you are holding onto. Ask your Heavenly Father to show you any areas in your heart that need to be enlightened so that your joy of receiving can be full. We all have areas of unforgiveness hiding that when we come before our Father He can plainly see where we are blind. Secondly unbelief, I ask you to consider for a moment, in the True Lord's Prayer that I have shared with you, do you believe everything he, Jesus, said and was asking the Father to do on your behalf or not? Next question for you, did Jesus get his prayers answered when he prayed or not? Once you allow these two issues to be brought to the light and life of the Word, your answers will flow freely because you have removed the logjam to your prayers.

    I can't end this chapter on Prayer without sharing also that sometimes we don't receive those answers to our prayers. Many a Saints, including the apostle Paul prayed that an issue be removed from him, and all he got for an answer was "My Grace is sufficient".

> *He said to me, "My grace is sufficient for you, for My strength is made perfect in weakness." Therefore most gladly I will rather boast of my infirmities, that the power of Christ may rest upon me.*
>
> *2 Corinthians 12:9*

    Not exactly, what he was expecting, and sometimes we hear the same thing over a situation that we are going through. However, what Paul said is quite profound. What we might think is an issue that needs to be healed, could often be a weakness in our body as that "blessing in disguise" so that the power of Christ may rest upon us as we minister to others. We can see this in the conversation Jesus had with his disciples in:

> *Now as Jesus passed by, He saw a man who was blind from birth. And His disciples asked Him, saying, "Rabbi, who sinned, this man or his parents, that he was born blind?*
>
> *Jesus answered, "Neither this man nor his parent sinned, but that the works of God should be revealed in him."*
>
> John 9:1–3

I say, don't quit praying over your situation. You never know what blow from the hammer of prayer, will conquer your obstacle has we can see through:

> *Then the Lord said, "Hear what the unjust judge said. And shall God not avenge His own elect who cry out day and night to Him, though He bears long with them? I tell you that He will avenge them speedily. Nevertheless, when the Son of Man comes, will He really find faith on the earth?"*
>
> Luke 17:6–8

Or might your situation be that "blessing in disguise" so that the power of Christ will rest upon you to allow His glory to be revealed through you and your situation either way...

ALWAYS BELIEVE WITH YOUR MOST ACTIVE AND HOLY FAITH!

Protecting Our Christian Identity

Our Christian Identity has been stolen from many in the Body of Christ today, and this isn't a recent happening. Our Christian identity was stolen from us many, many years ago; beginning at the Cross that Christ hung on. Through this chapter, we will begin to see that neither Jesus nor God intended us to be in this life alone, regardless of what the devil has led many to believe. In order to know if you have lost something, you first need to know that you had it. A thief wants to keep you from protecting and sharing your identity. First thing that we need to understand is just how our Christian Identity was been stolen from us, and secondly how can we restore our identity.

Let's begin by looking back at the day that Christ was crucified. That day, every one of Christ disciples abandoned Him with the exception of John, Jesus' mother Mary, Mary the wife of Clopas, and Mary Magdalene as told to us in:

> *Now there stood by the cross of Jesus His mother, and His mother's sister, Mary the wife of Clopas, and Mary Magdalene. When Jesus therefore saw His mother, and the disciple who He loved standing by, He said to His mother, "Woman, behold your son! Then He said to the*

> disciple, *"Behold your mother! And from that hour that disciple took her to his own home.*
>
> *John 19:25–27*

None of the other disciples were there at the cross that day because of fear of what was happening to Jesus would happen to them. They each had their own perceptions of what Jesus was talking about to them regarding the Kingdom of God and His Kingdom, and now that somehow wasn't going to happen since He was being crucified for His teachings. Even the words Jesus spoke on the cross that day;

> *And about the ninth hour Jesus cried out with a loud voice, saying, "Eli, Eli, lama sabachthani?" that is "My God, My God, why have You forsaken Me.?"*
>
> *Matthew 27:46*

Rings in the minds of many Christians as they are enduring hardships. This is but one of the tactics that the enemy, the devil, uses against us whenever we are going through the trying times in which we live. Somehow, we have understood that to be a Christian, we will never have to endure anything bad ever again, which is simply untrue. What is true is that while we are going through "stuff", Jesus will never leave us, just as our Father God, never left or forsook Jesus that day.

Now you say, Ok, if the disciples with the exception of John weren't at the cross, then where were they? Good question and I am glad you asked it, they were off hiding, because of what was happening to Jesus. Each of them believed that they were going to be something great in a new kingdom government that was going to take over the ruling kingdom government of their day. When they saw that Jesus was being crucified for His teachings, their hopes for fame and glory from a new kingdom government were dashed, and they now were falling back and regrouping so to speak. Jesus even warned the disciples that when the Shepherd was struck, the sheep would scatter.

> *The Jesus said to them, "All of you will be made to stumble because of Me this night, for it is written: I will strike the Shepherd, And the sheep of the flock will be scattered."*
>
> Matthew 26:31

This is simply human nature. We all have a flight or fight response to situations around us, and had anyone of us been there that day, we would have done as most of the disciples did. RUN AWAY! In this flight response however, there is a Spirit of an Orphan attached to it. The Orphan Spirit is one that feels totally alone and left to themselves in this world, and this is exactly what the disciples were dealing with that day. They felt alone, felt that they had nothing to fight with or for any longer and somehow that they didn't belong to anyone anymore and had to hide for their own safety because their Shepherd had been struck down. Little did they remember that Jesus also told them that He would see them later as we see in the scripture:

> *"But after I have been raised, I will go before you to Galilee."*
>
> Matthew 26:32

This Spirit of an Orphan attaches to us when we first become a born-again Child of God, because the enemy, the devil still tries to maintain his hold on us, by trying to convince us that we are alone, and that somehow God has now forsaken us until we get to Heaven. Not that he can take you out of God's hand, however, if he can keep you from realizing your full potential as a Child of God, then he has quelled the Spirit within you to become less effective in your everyday life, and will cause you not to share your faith and Christian Identity with anyone else. This is exactly what the enemy has done to a vast majority of Christians today. Many don't want to get into discussions with anyone because they don't want to become persecuted for their beliefs.

Your full potential as a Child of God is one of a son or daughter, NOT an orphan. Once you begin to fully recognize and understand your Christian Identity, and how the enemy is trying to keep you from your full potential, then you will begin walking in the confidence of a son or daughter and shed that Spirit of an orphan mentality. Let's begin by looking at how an orphan sees God, and we will finish up this chapter by showing you how a son or daughter views Him.

Orphan Mentality

An orphan will see God as a hard taskmaster, always seeking to somehow not to make God angry. The only way to describe this is how the black slaves that were forced into slavery by their white landlords. The slaves were often beaten into submission, and this is what an orphan Christian feels about his God. An orphan sees himself as a worthless nothing that deserves to be punished and scolded at every turn.

Once an orphan Christian works out of the slave mentality of their belief system, they will feel that they are completely independent of the need for a Higher authority, and will often tell you that they are self-made, and can handle things on their own. They believe that they don't need anyone or anything added to their life, and as a result will become very arrogant in their way that they handle their lives.

Orphans love to live by rules and regulations instead of relying on the law of love and compassion. Many times, they will be the Christians that are most prone to beating you over the head with their bible and scriptures. Many times these orphan Christians will condemn other Christians for not living a pious enough life. They will also debate as to whether these believers are truly Christians. Their only definition of grace is what you are to say before your meals.

Orphans will always display a lack of security and peace in their life, because they feel that if they don't control every situation around them, then they are completely out of control. If an orphan Christian isn't in control of their environment then they become very secluded and many times will become those religious zealots that live alone somewhere, thinking that they are protecting themselves from the evils of the world outside.

When orphan Christians are around others they will always seek for the approval of those around him or her to give them the recognition that they need to feel complete. They will often times seek out other's praise in an attempt to make themselves feel better about themselves and their life. Orphans only seek to serve themselves in any given situation, and never consider serving someone else. Orphans are highly "works" oriented, thinking that somehow if they do enough "good works" that they are earning their keep with God and as a Christian.

Most Christians that we see today that are extremely "Holy" or "devout" have lost their true identity that Christ came to give them. They are the type of Christians that must walk around with a "woe is me" or "unworthy" attitude to somehow feel that they are gaining God's favor for being so. Many times these Christians will feel that they just don't measure up to those that they regard as more "holy" than they are, and with that feeling comes the shame and guilt because they are somehow being rejected for not being as holy or devout as others.

Orphan Christians are the ones that will seek their comfort with other things in life. Those comforts can come from a wide range of things from being addicted to drugs or mind altering forms of meditation, being over achievers in everything that they do, to being hyper-religious. All of these avenues of seeking to comfort one's self are clues that this person is living with an orphan mentality.

Every time an orphan minded Christian becomes involved with other Christians, they feel as if they are in competition with their peers. They see themselves as being in competition with everyone that they are around, regardless of how the others may view the situation. They have to be the best, and will become jealous towards others within their peer group if they feel that they haven't received the recognition of how good they are, or how much better they are than others within the group are. Orphans will always seek to tear others down by building themselves up. They can very rarely if ever acknowledge that someone else had a better way, or achieved something that they have not. These types of Christians will always bring the topic of conversation back around to them and what they have or are doing. The can never be happy for someone else's success. Neither can they show compassion when others need comforting. Mercy is not in there vocabulary or in their mindset.

Orphan minded Christians always sees people that are in authority as a source of their own pain and will avoid them at almost any cost. They are very distrustful of anyone who seems to be over them in position or rank, and can never come under that authority because of their own insecurities. They cannot take correction from anyone, and if someone does try to correct their behavior, attitude, or misinterpretation then they will always go on the defensive side of the topic. They will try to justify their actions, and will never understand why they are being corrected.

Orphan Christian Mentality sees God as being in a faraway place called Heaven, and sees Him as being very uncaring or uninvolved in the daily grind of life. They can't grasp the concept that God is right here and now, in every moment of every day of their lives. They see God's love as being conditioned upon how they act, think or feel, and never will acknowledge Him as truly being a loving, caring compassionate Father because in their minds humans are not worthy of that type of relationship with the Almighty God.

Orphans are the type Christians that believe that you should strive for everything that you can get, can all you can get, and sit on the can to protect it. They live in a constant state of bondage, and freedom is just another word for nothing left to lose because they feel that they are nothing, they have nothing and never will be anything except the lowly worm that they feel that they are.

Orphan mentality is all too often the result of these people's past. They will be the ones that have come out of abusive situations in their life. They have actually been programmed into this way of thinking, over the course of many years of abuse. The abuse could be chemical, physical, emotional, sexual, or just out and out neglect in their life. Often times it will be a combination of these factors and will require patience on the part of anyone willing to step up or step into these orphan minded Christian's lives to show them their true identity as a son or daughter of the Most High Father God!

Spirit of a Son/Daughter

The Spirit of a son or daughter is not really something that can be taught but rather must be caught. Nevertheless, we have a guide by which to receive this mighty and freeing revelation. That guide being the Word of God. In understanding our true identity, we must believe and receive that identity. Just as you believe that, you are the child of your parents, whether biological or adopted. Your parents didn't have to convince you that you were their child, no more than they had to convince you that the house that you live is your house.

The Spirit of a son or daughter is actually referred to in the bible as the Spirit of Adoption. God's plan "A" was always ADOPTION, and He never had a plan "B". We gain our first insight into this Spirit of Adoption in the first scripture that you probably ever heard prior to become a born again Christian.

> *For God so loved the world that He gave His only begotten Son, that whoever believe in Him should not perish but have everlasting life.*
>
> *John 3:16*

Notice if you will that God was the first parent that ever willing gave their child up for adoption and in so doing was looking for other children through that gift He so willing gave. Many Christian ministers will say, God sowed the seed of His Son, so that He could receive many more Sons and Daughters. Regardless of how you look at it, God gave first, so that you and I had an entrance into His family.

> *"I will be a Father to you, And you shall be My sons and daughters, Say the LORD Almighty."*
>
> *2 Corinthians 6:18*

Children of God with the right perspective on their identity will have received the promise of our Heavenly Father as stated in the following scripture that the Apostle Paul wrote down for us in:

> *That is, those who are the children of the flesh, these are not all children of God; but the children of the promise are counted as the seed.*
>
> *Romans 9:8*

Notice if you will that as you read just one scripture before Romans 9:8 Paul shows us that just because you might have been born into a family by linage, doesn't mean that you are a True Child, and therefore are subject to being disowned. However, a child through the Promised One, that is Jesus, can never be disowned because they are counted as the seed, just as Jesus was The Seed that was sown to receive you. An interesting fact about adoption in the natural sense, which backs up what we are saying regarding the Spiritual Adoption of us as Children of God, is that children that have been adopted into a natural family and by the laws of the land can never be disowned. Natural children of two parents can be disowned from inheriting anything of their parents, but the law looks at adopted children differently because they were Chosen, not receive through reproductive means.

> *Blessed be the God and Father of our Lord Jesus Christ, who has blessed us with every spiritual blessing in the heavenly places in Christ, just as He chose us in Him before the foundation of the world, that we should be holy and without blame before Him in love, having predestined us to adoption as sons by Jesus Christ to Himself, according to the good pleasure of His will, to the praise of the glory of His grace, by which He made us accepted in the Beloved.*
>
> *Ephesians 1:3–6*

> *But as many as received Him, to them He gave the right to become children of God, to those who believe in His name; who were born, not of blood, nor of the will of the flesh, nor of the will of man, but of God.*
>
> *John 1:12 & 13*

> *For as many as are led by the Spirit of God, these are sons of God. For you did not receive the spirit of bondage again to fear, but you received the Spirit of Adoption by whom we cry out, "Abba, Father." The Spirit Himself bears witness with our spirit that we are children of God, and if children, then heirs—heirs of God and joint*

heirs with Christ if indeed we suffer with Him that we may also be glorified together.

Romans 8:14–17

Now, I say that the heir, as long as he is a child, does not differ at all from a slave, though he is master of all, but is under guardians and stewards until the time appointed by the father. Even so we, when we were children, were in bondage under the elements of the world. But when the fullness of the time had come, God sent forth His Son, born of a woman, born under the law, to redeem those who were under the law, that we might receive the adoption as sons. And because you are sons, God has sent forth the Spirit of His Son into your hearts, crying out, "Abba, Father!" Therefore you are no longer a slave but a son, and if a son, then an heir of God through Christ.

Galatians 4: 1–6

Behold what manner of love the Father has bestowed on us, that we should be called children of God! Therefore the world does not know us, because it did not know Him.

1 John 3:1

Adopted sons and daughters of God live their life by the Law of Love, Grace and Peace, they don't get entangled with who is or who isn't a Christian, and their service to others is always done in the love that God has for them. Serving others, and seeing to the needs of others before their own is always a first priority with children of God that hold within themselves their true identity as children of God.

Sons and daughters of God are quite content to find alone time, just so that they can rest in their Father's presence and loving adoration. They don't mind the quiet times because in those quiet times alone with God, are the most rewarding and fulfilling times in their life. This is a time that they receive the refreshing of their spirits so that they can go back out and serve others as their Heavenly Father asks, and in these quiet times are when their cups are filled to overflowing with love that can be pour out onto others.

Mature sons and daughters of God will always rejoice with others regarding success in those others may have. They will never demonstrate a spirit of envy when things are happening for others. They truly walk in a humble spirit knowing that God loves them, and their success is just around the corner from them, if it isn't for them right now. They will always keep a positive and affirming attitude towards others success, and will be the first to mourn and weep with someone who just needs a shoulder to bear their burdens on.

Mature sons and daughters of God with their true identities, intact will receive correction from others without feeling attacked or persecuted. They will evaluate every correction from those in authority over them, and discuss their issues privately with God to learn the lessons that they need. The bible says that God loves His children and He will correct those whom need correction, as we can see in the scriptures.

> *You should know in your heart that as a man chastens his son, so the LORD you God chastens you.*
>
> *Deuteronomy 8:5*

My son, do not despise the chastening of the LORD, *Nor detest His corrections; For whom the* LORD *loves He corrects, Just as a father the son in whom he delights.*

Proverbs 3:11 & 12

If you endure chastening, God deals with you as with sons; for what son is there who a father does not chasten? But if you are without chastening, of which all have become partakers, then you are illegitimate and not sons. Furthermore, we have had human fathers who corrected us, and we paid them respect. Shall we not much more readily be in subjection to the Father of spirits and live.

Hebrews 12:7–9

Christians with a proper identity in their standing with God will always view Him as a loving, caring, compassionate Father. Regardless of whether they had a loving, caring compassionate natural Father, their Heavenly Father will be so real to them, that no one will ever convince them that they aren't loved and cared for by Him.

Knowing and understanding our rights as children of God, we will always see a need for Him in our life. Life without a loving and compassionate Father God is really no life at all to a Christian with right perspective of their Heavenly Father. Just as when you were a child living in your parent's home, you were dependent upon them for everything in your life. So too is the Child of God dependent upon all the blessings and benefits that flow to them from their Heavenly Father. A Christian with the proper perspective on their identity as a child of God will always acknowledge and seek out God's assistance with everything in their life.

Now I pray that each of you receives, and has caught the Spirit of Adoption as sons and daughters of our Heavenly Father. I pray that you be imitators of God as His dear children. I pray that you walk in love even as Christ your elder brother has and in which He willing gave Himself as an offering and a sacrifice for us, as a sweet smelling aroma unto God. May the revelation knowledge of your true identity as God's own children guide your spirit into your full inheritance as partakers of that inheritance with Jesus. AMEN!

Kingdom Experience

The most important message that Jesus came to give to man was about The Kingdom of God. In the day that Jesus came to this earth, He was preaching about the Kingdom of God and how that we were to seek The Kingdom of God and His Righteousness first. As the central theme to Jesus' message is why we have placed His message directly in the middle of our handbook. We have done this to serve as a reminder to all who read this chapter and learn the lessons contained within the other chapters, that the central theme to all of our faith is seeking first the Kingdom of God and His Righteousness. It is also the least understood of any principles, however the simplest one we can wrap our minds around it. Through Jesus' own words, and a little light shown upon His word, you will see that you to have the Kingdom of God within you, and now just allow that Kingdom to grow, thrive, and consume the very fabric of your being. Throughout the New Testament of the Bible we find that the message regarding The Kingdom of God is spoken of 69 times, and The Kingdom of Heaven is spoken of 32 times. For the purpose of this chapter however, we will only be examining a few of these scriptures in detail to help simplify your understanding on The Kingdom of God and Heaven, so that you may share it with others using the K.I.S.S. (Keep It Simple Stupid) Method of teaching.

Throughout Jewish history, the Jewish people had been expecting God to restore the glory of Israel and to put an end to their enemies that sought their demise. So when John the Baptist and then Jesus entered the scene, a new and better kingdom was understood to be coming, however, they expected it to be an earthly type kingdom with which they understood. However, the Kingdom that Jesus came to set up was a spiritual Kingdom, which would grow from within the hearts of men and women, and would have the sovereign Rule of God to defeat all the evil powers that are at work within the world of then and now.

Several times, it is mentioned, in the bible that Jesus compared the Kingdom of God to be like a seed that a farmer would plant into the ground. It would spring up, and grow, and produce a crop, many times the amount that was sown. Such is the Kingdom of God within our hearts; Jesus' message of the Kingdom is planted deep within the soil of our hearts as believers in His Word. As the message grows and multiplies the living Word of God and His message begins to consume the heart and minds of all His believers which will then spread the message of the Kingdom throughout their spheres of influence within the world. This is how the Kingdom of God is built, and walks throughout this earth, by Revelation and Relationship through all our spheres of influence. The following scriptures are directly from Jesus' message about the Kingdom, which is our proof of what we are discussing in this chapter.

> *Then He spoke many things to them in parables saying: "Behold, a sower went out to sow. And as he sowed, some seed fell by the wayside; and the birds came and devoured them. Some fell on stony places, where they did not have much earth; and they immediately sprang*

up because they had no depth of earth. But when the sun was up they were scorched, and because they had no root they withered away. And some fell among thorns, and the thorns sprang up and choked them. But others fell on good ground and yielded a crop; some a hundredfold, some sixty, some thirty. He who has ears to hear, let him hear!"

Matthew 13:3–9

"Therefore hear the parable of sower; When anyone hears the word of the kingdom, and does not understand it, they the wicked one comes and snatches away what was sown in his heart. This is he who received seed by the wayside. But he who received the seed on stony places, this is he who hears the word and immediately receive it with joy; yet he has no root in himself, but endures only for a while. For when tribulations or persecution arises because of the word, immediately he stumbles. Now he who received seed among the thorns is he who hears the word, and the cares of this world and the deceitfulness of riches choke the word, and he becomes unfruitful. But he who received seed on the good ground is he who hears the word and understand it, who indeed bears fruit and produces; some a hundredfold, some sixty, some thirty."

Matthew 13: 18–23

Jesus fully explains how the Kingdom of God grows, spreads, and reproduces in the above referenced scriptures. However when as a Christian believer, just starting out into the Ministry, I needed a little further information regarding this subject, and the Holy Spirit simplified it even further for my simplistic brain as follows: He instructed me to look around at the congregation seated in the sanctuary of the church one day, and spoke this to my heart. "You see these people sitting in the chairs, start counting 1, 2, 3, 4, and every fourth one is one that will receive and reproduce the words that I will have you speak. One out of every four will be good ground." The words that the Holy Spirit spoke to my heart that day gave me such Joy and Peace, knowing that yes, not everyone would reproduce what I was speaking to them about the Kingdom and God's word, just as every seed that I sowed in my vegetable garden would produce a crop. However, just as I didn't stop sowing seed in my garden year after year, neither should I stop sowing the Word of God into the hearts that passed by me year after year. So readers, neither should you be discouraged when you feel like your message is falling on deaf ears, and just continue to sow knowing that one out of every four will produce a crop, some hundred, some sixty, some thirtyfold results, all credited to your account as the harvest is brought into the Kingdom of God.

For the sake of making it easier for the reader of this chapter, we are only going to list the scripture references of these 69 references for your future study on the subject.

Scripture References for The Kingdom of God:

Matthew 6:33; Matthew 12:28; Matthew 19:24; Matthew 21:31; Matthew 21:43; Mark 1:14 & 15; Mark 4:11; Mark 4:26; Mark 4:30; Mark 9:1; Mark 9:47; Mark 10:14 & 15; Mark 10:23–25; Mark 12:34; Mark 14:25; Mark 15:43; Luke 4:43; Luke 6:20; Luke 7:28; Luke 8:1; Luke 8:10; Luke 9:2; Luke 9:11; Luke 9:27; Luke 9:60; Luke 9:62; Luke 10:9; Luke 10:11; Luke 11:20; Luke 12:31; Luke 13:18; Luke 13:20; Luke 13:28 & 29; Luke 14:15; Luke 16:16; Luke 17:20 & 21; Luke 18:16 & 17; Luke 18:24 & 25; Luke 18:29; Luke 19:11; Luke 21:31; Luke 22:16 &18; Luke

23:51; John 3:3 & 5; Acts 1:3; Acts 8:12; Acts 14:22; Acts 19:8; Acts 20:25; Acts 28:23; Acts 28:31; Romans 14:17; 1 Corinthians 4:20; 1 Corinthians 6:9 & 10; 1 Corinthians 15:50; Galatians 5:21; Colossians 4:11; 2 Thessalonians 1:5;

We have also listed the scripture references for The Kingdom of Heaven, which in most cases throughout the bible are used interchangeably. There are 32 references of the Kingdom of Heaven mentioned in addition to the 69 Kingdom of God references, for your further study and understanding.

Scripture References for The Kingdom of Heaven:

Matthew 3:2; Matthew 4:17; Matthew 5:3, 5 10, 19,20; Matthew 7:21; Matthew 8:11; Matthew 10:7; Matthew 11:11, 12; Matthew 13:11, 24, 31, 33, 44, 45, 47, 52; Matthew 16:19; Matthew 18:1, 3, 4, 23; Matthew 19:12, 14, 23; Matthew 20:1; Matthew 22:2; Matthew 23:13; Matthew 25:1, 14

Dear Heavenly Father, I pray that through your Word and your dear Son Jesus, and the doors to understanding Your Kingdom, the Kingdom of God opens wide within my heart and the hearts to all that will cross my path today. In Jesus' Name AMEN!

Understanding Our Righteousness Through Christ

If there is one subject that seems to take our brains and twist them, just a little is the subject of a believer being the righteousness of God. All believers are Righteous regardless of their sinful past or what sins they may commit in the future. Therefore, that is exactly why we have included this subject within our handbook, to help explain your righteous standing so that you can fully explain the subject to others in your sphere of influence.

Let's begin by examining the words righteous and righteousness: These two words are repeated throughout the New Testament of the bible, and are often the most overlooked words as Christians read their bibles, simply because they have not grasped the full understanding of their righteousness that obtained through their believing on the Lord Jesus Christ as their savior. Many Christians think that their savior only saved them from the fires of Hell; however, our salvation was much more than that as we will see throughout this chapter.

Righteousness is an instantaneous condition of every believer the moment they are BORN-AGAIN. At the new birth, the believer receives the NATURE of our righteous Heavenly Father God. The new believer receives God's Righteousness.

> But now the righteousness of God apart from the law is revealed, being witnessed by the Law and the Prophets, even the righteousness of God, through faith in Jesus Christ, to all and on all who believe. For there is no difference,
>
> Romans 3: 21–22

Righteousness is the ability to stand in prayer or in the presence of The Almighty, Holy God, as if you had never sinned or heard of sin. You old sinful nature before you receive Jesus as your savior is no longer standing as a GUILTY SIGN, between you and God. You are, and have been judged, RIGHTEOUS just as you have never sinned, or been a sinner. Jesus paid the full price!

> For all have sinned and fall short of the glory of God, being justified freely by His grace through the redemption that is in Christ Jesus, whom God set forth as a propitiation by His blood, through faith, to demonstrate His righteousness, because in His forbearance God had passed over the sins that were previously committed, to demonstrate at the present time His righteousness, that He might be just and the justifier of the one who has faith in Jesus.
>
> Romans 3: 23–26

Righteousness is being able to stand before God without any fear or inferiority. You are a child of God once you have accepted the FREE gift of righteousness through Jesus' payment.

> Now it was not written for his sake alone that it was imputed to him, but also for us. It shall be imputed to us who believe in Him who raised up Jesus our Lord from

> *the dead, who was delivered up because of our offenses, and was raised because of our justification.*
>
> Romans 4:23–25

Righteousness is the ability to stand before God as a Son, greatly beloved and approved by our Heavenly Father God. When you accepted Jesus' payment, the Spirit of Adoption has transformed you into a child of God. This was always your heavenly Father's Plan A to receive you into His family as a Son or Daughter of the most High.

> *Blessed be the God and Father of our Lord Jesus Christ, who has blessed us with every spiritual blessing in the heavenly places in Christ, just as He chose us in Him before the foundation of the world, that we should be holy and without blame before Him in love, having predestined us to adoption as sons by Jesus Christ to Himself, according to the good pleasure of His will, to the praise of the glory of His grace, by which He made us accepted in the Beloved.*
>
> Ephesians 1:3–6

Righteousness is a condition entered into only through FAITH, and cannot be accomplished by a man or woman's own good works, or good deeds that they may do. It is only by our faith in Jesus, and what He did for us that can ever make us righteous. Only through faith in Jesus are we declared righteous, and nothing else. The requirement is only faith, and many teach that you have to have good works to be righteous and that is simply NOT TRUE according to the word of God. You were created FOR GOOD WORKS; your righteousness IS NOT created BY YOUR GOOD WORKS.

> *For by grace you have been saved through faith, and that not of yourselves; it is the gift of God, not of works, lest anyone should boast. For we are His workmanship, created in Christ Jesus for good works, which God prepared beforehand that we should walk in them.*
>
> *Ephesians 2: 8–10*

Righteousness could and was only accomplished for man through the work of the Lord Jesus Christ in His death, burial, and resurrection. Furthermore, righteousness means that we can go to God in prayer and praise just like Adam and Eve did prior to their sin, with NO CONDEMNATION! You are a child of God, and once you accepted Jesus' finished work will remain a child of God.

> *There is therefore now no condemnation to those who are in Christ Jesus, who do not walk according to the flesh, but according to the Spirit.*
>
> *Romans 8:1*

God created the New Creation man in righteousness and true holiness as we can read in the Ephesians 4:24, therefore, as that New creation created by God, you are now and have never been a sinner! God destroyed the old nature the moment that you accepted Jesus into your heart and you were made completely brand new, with a clean slate as His righteous son or daughter. Through your righteousness which is through Jesus Christ, you too can do all the things that Jesus did, and greater works shall you do, because Jesus has gone to the Father on your behalf. As the New Creation Man or Woman of God, you are greatly feared by the enemy, the devil, and have Christ's and God's ability residing within you.

> "Most assuredly, I say to you, he who believes in Me, the works that I do he will do also; and greater works than these he will do, because I go to My Father.
>
> *John 14:12*

Becoming conscious of the Righteousness that is yours, as a believer will have the following DYNAMIC, LIFE-CHANGING effects upon your life:

1. Righteous Consciousness will set you free from the sense of guilt and shame that you once had before you became a Born-Again Child of God.

2. Righteous Consciousness will establish within your heart and mind your worthiness to stand before God.

3. Righteous Consciousness will give you knowledge that you are truly accepted in the Beloved by God.

4. Righteous Consciousness will produce peace in your life and home as it becomes engrained into your everyday thinking and reactions.

5. Righteous Consciousness will cause you to have a willing and receptive heart to receive all that your Father God has for you.

6. Righteous Consciousness will cause oppression and depression to become a thing of your past, and no longer in your future.

7. Righteous Consciousness will drive fear and torment far away from you, your mind, and your life.

8. Righteous Consciousness will give you confidence and boldness in prayer and when dealing with others in your sphere of influence like you have never had before.

9. Righteous Consciousness will cause your faith to explode into victory within every area of your life.//
10. Righteous Consciousness is the power and force that will stop sin and will cause right actions to follow instead of wrong ones.

I will share a personal example of how dramatic a difference your life will become when you become consciously aware of your righteousness and right standing with God. As a young Christian, at the age of 26 years old, I was never taught that I as a believer I was now in right standing with God as if I had never sinned. I came from a very orthodox Pentecostal background, where every Sunday and Wednesday we would all have to renew our faith in Jesus to maintain our salvation. If we didn't we would surely be going to hell for some wrong thoughts, wrong actions that we might have committed while we were traveling through our daily lives and somehow that caused us to lose our salvation between Church services. We were even condemned as a sinner if we were wearing something that didn't make us look like little old ladies in moo moos that covered every inch of our bodies. Shorts and pants were out of the question for women, and don't even get me started on the fact that your hair could never be cut, or you were simply out of the will of God, and headed straight to hell for sure. One day, I started attending another Church, because I just didn't seem to adjust to the lifestyle requirement of my previous church. The first sermon that I heard in that new church was a teaching on this particular subject that we have been discussing in this chapter. I was created righteous the first day that I accepted Jesus into my heart. What a novel concept. Nothing I could ever do from that point on would make me righteous or keep me in right standing in God's eyes, I already was righteous and there wasn't any way that I could lose my righteous standing as His Child once I believed. No rule of man or man-made religions has kept me as His Child; I was adopted as His child period.

Once this new found revelation entered into my conscious mind and began to grow, and expand, I became less afraid of what was lurking around the next corner, I became more loving, caring and compassionate for others, and most of all became more accepting of myself, and the way that God had created me. All of these and many more benefits grew and developed through the years as I became freer and freer within my relationship with My Heavenly Father. I realized that He wasn't mad at me, He enjoyed my company and companionship during our quiet times alone, and that He even laughs over my enemies who try to overtake my life or my mind. Once you are a child of God, nothing and no one can ever take you out of His hand. The scripture that solidified this understanding for me is found in:

> *But thus says the LORD: "Even the captives of the mighty shall be taken away, And the prey of the terrible be delivered; For I will contend with him who contends with you, And I will save your children. I will feed those who oppress you with their own flesh, And they shall be drunk with their own blood as with sweet wine. All flesh shall know That I, the LORD, am your Savior, And your Redeemer, the Mighty One of Jacob."*
>
> *Isaiah 49:25–26*

Dear Heavenly Father, I now know and understand that I am your child, and that you have made me righteous. I am in right standing with you because I believe and have accepted what your Son Jesus did for me. I am not righteous by my own doing; you made me righteous when I accepted the finished work that Jesus did on the cross that day long ago. I can never do anything more than accept your righteousness that you have given me and rest in that righteousness as your child. In Jesus' Name, AMEN!

Overview of the Spiritual Gifts

Whether you call them the gifts of the spirit or spiritual gifts, the subject has always been a hotly debated subject within the Christian community. As any natural loving parent wants to provide gifts to their children, why should our Heavenly Father be any different? Therefore, why should there be such debate surrounding the fact that He wants us to benefit and have His children edified by those gifts? The debate is spurred by the very sad fact that most Christians today don't have a proper understanding of the Spiritual Gifts that have been provided, nor do they understand that these specific gifts are meant for the help and welfare of the entire body of Christ known as "The Church". For this subject "The Church" is not a building that you go to, it is what you are as a believer in Jesus, all members of ONE body of believers. Spiritual Gifts are as we will discuss for the building up of "The Church" body, and shouldn't be confusing, misunderstood, or neglected.

In 1 Corinthians chapter 12 we find that spiritual gifts are given to the people of God by the Holy Spirit for the over-all welfare and common benefit of all. They are given according to God's will, as He decides, and are for the preparation of His people for serving and building or strengthening the body of Christ called The Church. Typically, the Gifts of the Spirit can be divided, into three different categories: Gifts of Ministry, Gifts of Manifestation, and Gifts of Motivation.

Gifts of Ministry

> *But to each one of us grace was given according to the measure of Christ's gift. There fore He says: "When He ascended on high, He led captivity captive, And gave gifts to men." [Now this, "He ascended"—what does it mean but that He also first descended into the lower parts of the earth? He who descended is also the One who ascended far above all the heavens, that He might fill all things]*
>
> *And He Himself gave some to be apostles, some prophets, some evangelists, and some pastor and teachers, for the equipping of the saints for the work of ministry, for the edifying of the body of Christ, till we all come to the unity of the faith and the knowledge of the Son of God, to a perfect man, to the measure of the stature of the fullness of Christ; that we should no longer be children, tossed to and fro and carried about with every wind of doctrine, by the trickery of men, in the cunning craftiness of deceitful plotting, but speaking the truth in love, may grow up in all things into Him who is the head—Christ—from whom the whole body, joined and knit together by what every joint supplies, according to the effective working by which every part does it share, causes growth of the body for the edifying of itself in love.*
>
> *Ephesians 4:7–16*

The gifts of ministry are given to reveal or put into action the Plans and purposes of God. Many times when we talk about spiritual gifts most assume that they are only for ministry application, however, as we will discuss, these gifts have practical business applications as well. Once we learn and apply these gifts to the whole spectrum of spiritual and practical applications, then we will begin to allow the Plan of God to flow through every area of our lives through these gifting's.

The Gift of Apostle: Is many times referred to as the THUMB of the ministry gifts. Just like the natural thumb on your hand pushes your peas on to your fork or knife, so too does the Apostle push all the necessary components of the ministry or business together, and fits them into place. This gift is what most church planters or entrepreneurs have been given, and as such the people that have been given this gift, will many time function in all the Spiritual Gifts providing assistance where needed within the other gifting. And just as you learned when you were a kid while thumb wrestling with your friends, it the strongest and most powerful finger on your hand, so to this is the strongest and most powerful spiritual gift, with the ability and talent to help all other gifts. These are also entrepreneurs that build and establish businesses within the business community as well as building and planting church or ministry organizations.

The Gift of Prophet: Surprising to many, Yes this Gift is still very much in operation today. However, this one gift is also the most often sought after gift by control freaks, and they try to manipulate others into believing they have been given the Gift of the Prophet when all they have ever been given is the give of manipulation and control, and that wasn't given by God, I can assure you. The Gift of the Prophet is the gift that is represented on your natural hand as the INDEX FINGER, or mister pointer. Just as mister pointer finger likes to point out everything, so too does the Gift of the Prophet. The Gift of the Prophet will point to the future of the people of God and will also point out where sin or problems reside. The Gift of the Prophet when manifested within the TRUE gift will be ACCURATE! The Gift of the Prophet when given by the Holy Spirit of God CANNOT BE WRONG. When you see someone operating in this spiritual gift, or should I say pretending to operate in this spiritual gift and they have missed their prediction or forecast of future events or identifying where sin or issues that need resolving is, this is never from God, and from such you should run, don't walk away. The Gift of the Prophet isn't like the Old Testament prophet pronouncing judgment, the New Testament Gift of the Prophet will always be edifying and uplifting in nature. One important distinction to be aware of when witnessing the Gift of the Prophet is that God's people win, and the only purpose that the Gift of the Prophet has in identifying where sin and issue reside is so that we can repent or change our minds regarding our failings, and continue in the will of God for our lives. A good rule of thumb for identifying this Gift as to whether it is from God or not; is to remember that when "Mister Point" is pointing to something that is true or not, there are three fingers always pointing back at him or herself.

The Gift of Evangelist: This gift is represented on our natural hand as the MIDDLE FINGER. It is the longest or tallest of all our fingers, and stands out among them all. This finger is also the one that seems to take some of the hardest hits like being stuck into places or the first one to get jammed in the car door. The ministry gift of Evangelist standouts out among the congregation, and takes the most hits of criticism within the congregation or local body of believers. This Gift of the Evangelist has been gifted to reach out and draw people into a local body of believers. The gift of the Evangelists can also be referred to as "A Salesman" they are the ones that are gifted to sell a product. If they are pretending to operate in this Gift without drawing them into a local body of believers or to a product sold by their business, and only drawing attention to themselves, then they are giving the "middle finger" to God, and from such steer clear at all costs.

The Gift of Pastor: This gift is many times referred to as the RING FINGER of the organization. The person that fills this role is married to and responsible for overseeing to the welfare of the people within a specific organization. In a business sense, this would be the business manager or supervisory position within the organization. This gift is for the shepherding of people within a specific congregation or group specifically gathered together for the sole purpose of care and nurturing the people of within a ministry or business. A pastor is not just the person that stands at the pulpit within our churches today, a pastor is anyone that has oversight and seeks for the welfare of the members. A pastor is responsible for nurturing, guiding, and protecting the members within the group. In the truest sense of the word pastor, they are to be caregivers of the flock. Whether that flock is a group gathered together for business purposes, ministry or the combination of business and ministry purposes, the pastor is the one who answers to God for how well the flock (group) thrives and survives. If more business owners would see that their talent for operating businesses and managing people was a pastoral gifting, then we wouldn't be in our current economic crisis.

Those that should have regarded their positions of care and oversight as a God given gift or ability would have seen to the care of the flock instead of the care of their own desires. This gift along with all of the other ministry gifts have true business applications that if applied would create a completely different business climate as well as would no longer create the need for Big Government to regulate them, and fill in the gap that their lack of responsibility has caused.

The Gift of Teacher: This gift is sometimes a shared gift with the gift of the pastor; however, it doesn't have to be. The teacher is one that is able to simplify difficult tasks or concepts into easy to understand instructions. The teacher's primary focus is on accurate information and detail to see that the concept is learned and understood, in order to be reproduced by the student or others that will perform a specific task or duty. The gift of a teacher will pick apart and reassemble the Word of Truth or a specific task in order for others to grasp the concept and achieve the goals desired.

Gifts of Manifestation

There are diversities of gifts, but the same Spirit. There are differences of ministries, but the same Lord. And There are diversities of activities, but it is the same God who works all in all. But the manifestation of the Spirit is given to each one for the profit of all: for to one is given the word of wisdom through the Spirit, to another the word of knowledge through the same Spirit, to another faith by the same Spirit, to another gifts of healings by the same Spirit, to another the working of miracles, to another prophecy, to another discerning of spirits, to another different kinds of tongues, to another the interpretation tongues. But one and the same

> *Sprit works all these things, distributing to each one individually as He wills.*
>
> 1 Corinthians 12:4–11

Gifts of manifestation are often broken down into three different sub categories as to their specific manifested presence of God's power that is revealed. The three categories are Speech (Spoken Gifts), Action (Doing Gifts), and Revelation (Revealing Gifts). Through these gifts, God's power is revealed within a local church body or within a business that thrives and produces God's Will on the earth. You may not be as able to distinguish these gifts within every business venture at first, they will reveal themselves over the course of time, and will always prove themselves to be a very valuable employee within that business environment. Within a local church body or business, you will see these people with these gifts are the ones that always have a plan of action for specific situations, will have a word of encouragement for the members, or will have the ability to understand something that seems to be difficult for everyone else to understand or comprehend. So as not to further complicate your understanding of this group of gifting's, we will only be discussing these gifts within a local church setting, and will not delve to deeply into the business applications of these manifestation gifts.

Spoken Gifts:

1. *Prophecy*—One who operates in this gift will be telling forth the Word of God for the purpose of building up or inspiring members of the congregation or organization to continue on their

course of action based upon the Word or Plan of God. This will always be an encouraging word to persevere through, consolation when problems have arisen, etc… In a business setting it could also manifest itself as a spoken direction that has not been considered in the situation, but when acted upon would create the desired effect that the members are desiring to be achieved.

2. *Speaking in Tongues:* This gifting is found most often within a church congregation setting, and will not normally be seen within a business setting. However, businesses that do incorporate prayer within their business meetings that had this specific gift come forth as a message that God wanted to present, and will ALWAYS have someone else within the congregation or meeting confirm this manifestation of God with the Interpretation in the known language of the group. This is a language NOT known or learned by the speaker of this gift, and will have a very authoritative sound to it. No interpretation into a known and understandable language, then one of two things have occurred, either the speaker didn't realized that it was a private prayer language NOT for public display and displayed their spiritual immaturity by presenting it as a gift of tongues, or it wasn't from God and was meant to serve as a distraction.

3. *Interpretation of Tongues:* With this gift, there will be someone else in the room or meeting that first manifested the Gift of Tongues. When the speaker with the Gift of Tongues has concluded their part of the message, the person with an interpretation of

that message that was given in an unknown language, will immediately begin to have an interpretation of what was said. They will speak it in a plain and known language for the other members of the group. These messages will always be encouraging, and will line up with the Word of God, and will NEVER dispute the Word of God that can be easily found in your bible.

Action Gifts:

1. *Gift of Faith:* This gift is first experienced by every believer to have faith regarding Believing God, His Word, and believing in His only begotten Son, Jesus. The gift of faith is the only gift that is given to all believers at least once. The continued manifestation of this gift is what the bible is referring to here, which is a supernatural Faith to believe God for the impossible in impossible situations such as the Gift of faith to believe and receive supernatural miracles performed by the Spirit of God, or a knowing and believing in God to perform such miracles. Through this particular gift, you will see a manifestation of the power of God to perform what the person has received faith for. This isn't a mere wishing or hoping, remembers this is an action gift and with action comes manifestation.

2. *Gift of Healing:* If there were one gift that seems to be the most controversial of the gifts of the Spirit, it would be this one. The reason for this is because it has been so abused within the Christian Charismatic realms and the one that many have used or should I

say abused into a Money Making Opportunity that leaves a bad taste in everyone's mouth whenever anyone says anything about this gift. With that being said, with the true manifestation of this gift will always be a true and pure heart of compassion that will precede the manifestation of this gift. This compassion will begin to well up from deep inside the person with this gift, to the point that they must take some type of action to release this gift to the person that they see needs healing for an aliment or condition. The action performed by the person with this gifting isn't really the important part; it is the obedience to what they are feeling led to act upon. It could be tears, prayer, the touching of a person in need of healing, or even the like Jesus did when He caused the blind man to receive his sight by placing mud on the eyes of the blind man and telling him to go wash it off as found in the book of John chapter 9 verse 7.

3. *Gift of Miracles:* This gift is the manifestation of things that have supernaturally occurred against all the laws of nature. This gift has actually caused the natural laws of nature to be suspended for the Will of God to become manifested within the natural realm of man.

Revelation Gifts:

1. *Word of Wisdom:* Simply put this gift manifests itself with the ability to apply a Godly principle or truth to achieve or demonstrate the wisdom of God in a given situation or circumstance. Often times this

gift is disguised as simply someone demonstrating wisdom beyond their years or learning, when in actuality it is a divine gift of the Spirit of God operating within them to reveal that wisdom for the benefit of others.

2. *Word of Knowledge:* This gift most often will operate in concert with the Gift of Wisdom. A word of knowledge is something that wasn't or couldn't have been known by natural means, and the Gift of Wisdom is how that knowledge is to be applied in a particular situation or circumstance.

3. *Discerning of Spirits:* This gift of the Spirit, is another one of those gifts that has a natural counterpart, called the Gift of Suspicion. With the true gift of discerning of spirits given by the Holy Spirit as a gift, one is able to discern whether the spirits involved in a situation or circumstance are good or evil, truthful or lying spirits, or genuinely prophetic or satanic in their origins. Many times with the manifestation of this gift, the person that operates within this gifting frequently will be able to tell immediately whether it is the Spirit of God or Holy, or a manifestation of evil disguising itself as being good or holy. With others that might not operate as frequently in this gifting, will many times doubt themselves until they become more familiar as to how this gift operates through them. And others that only have the natural gift of human nature will operate in the gift of suspicion and be suspicious of everyone and everything, which is never from the Spirit of God and is only human and sometimes demonic in nature.

Gifts of Motivation

Having then gifts differing according to the grace that is given to us, let us use them: if prophecy, let us prophesy in proportion to our faith; or ministry, let us use it in our ministering; he who teaches, in teaching; he who exhorts, in exhortation; he who gives, with liberality; he who leads, with diligence; he who shows mercy, with cheerfulness.

Romans 12:6–8

Just as the title of this section suggest, the following gifts are what is known as gifts of motivation, or more simple said, what motivates an individual. These gifts just as the others that we have already discussed, are not given to everyone, however, everyone has one or several gifting's that motivates them into action each and every day of their lives. Just as all individuals are different in their personalities, these motivation gifts reveal the personality of our Heavenly Father as to whom he has given these gifts to, as well as how those gift function within each individual. With three questions that I will often ask, I can determine what motivates an individual, and where their gifting's lie. As we discuss the gifts of motivation, please keep these three questions in mind as you read, and you too will be able to easily determine yours and others gifts of motivation that our Heavenly Father has bestowed on you and those whom you work with on a daily basis. In our many ministry/businesses, we take this process one step further and have every employee take a spiritual gifts test, to determine with greater focus the gifts of motivation within each of our employees. When people are working in their specific areas of their God given gifts and abilities you have happier and more fulfilled employees, and these individuals are set up for success rather than failure.

THREE QUESTIONS TO DETERMINE YOUR MOTIVATION GIFTS:

1. What have you done in any particular day in your life that has given you the greatest satisfaction that you have had a GREAT day?
2. What gives you the greatest sense of accomplishment?
3. What annoys or irritates you the most when dealing with people?

These questions are just a quick way to find the most obvious gifts that you may have in operation through you. However, before you start claiming a gift that operates through you, it is best to invest a small amount of money and take any one of a number of Spiritual Gifts testing that can be found online. I must also tell you that more time than not, you might not operate in the same gift in different situations. The Spiritual Gift tests results can and will change over the years as to what you are currently involved with. Example: A pastor friend of mine didn't even register as a missionary on the Gifts Testing until about a year before the Lord sent him and his family to England.

Prophecy

The motive gift of prophecy is revealed within those individuals that tend to have insight into particular situations for which they may or may not be trained in. These people are many times referred to as the guard dogs of any organization because they can often times sense or see where issues are or will be within a given organization. These people are known as the "eyes" of the organization and as such can alert management or leadership as to problems many times before they become out of control.

Teaching

The motive gift of teacher or teaching is revealed within those individuals that enjoy training others in the subject matter at hand within an organization. They will be the ones that can take complex issues, projects, or subject and break them down into bite size nuggets of information so that everyone can comprehend the matter being taught and they will have a firm grasp of the lessons taught by an individual with this motivational gift. Individuals with this motive gifting is sometimes referred to as the "brains or the mind" of the operation.

Exhortation or Gift of Encouragement

The motive gift of exhortation is revealed in individuals that can speak persuasively which will cause an action to be taken by the one spoken too. These people are ones that will give advice or counsel to others. They are often times seen as the "mouthpiece" of the organization.

Gift of Giving

The motive gift of giving doesn't just mean the giving of money however that is one facet of this gift. Other facets of this gifting that will be revealed within individuals motivated by this gift can also include; random acts of kindness just because that is their nature, giving of their time, energy, talents or abilities, or simply the giving of themselves to others in times of need. The individual with this gift of giving will seem to irritate others because others will feel that a GIVER is only trying to give their way into heaven, or even to "suck up" to the boss. Givers are often times seen as the "arms" of any organization, which help to hold things up. Arms are limbs of the body that can help stabilize others by just their presence and giving nature.

Gift of Leadership

Many times this gift is referred to as the gift of administration or as; we have titled it according to the bible, the Gift of Leadership. The person that has this gifting will be very detail oriented, and seek to find ways to make the overall project, or organization run smoothly and efficiently. These people are good organizers and planners. Individuals displaying this gift will many times not choose to be in a leadership capacity, however if there is a vacancy in leadership, they will be the ones that will rise to the responsibility to fill the void. Their greatest sense of accomplishment comes from having a group of people come together to complete a task or project. These people represent the "head" of the body in which they are joined to. The head of the body will do whatever it believes is best for the body as a whole.

Gift of Mercy

Individuals that are gifted with the gift of mercy will be very sensitive to the needs of other individuals. These people are very extreme in their emotions, which can turn on a dime given the people that they are around. They are the ones that will laugh with you, cry with you, and seek to help anyone at a possible determent to themselves. Individuals with this gift are attracted to individuals that are in some sort of need or distress. Many times these people will not recognize when others are abusing their mercy-filled nature, and will many times become victims themselves when all they were trying to do is to help someone else. People with the gift of mercy are known as the "heart or heart beat" of an organization. They are led by their emotional needs to give mercy, regardless of the truth or the situation around them.

Gift of Ministry or Gift of Service

People with this gift of ministry are the doers of any organization. They don't want to sit around and wait for decisions to be made, they see a need, and they go do it. These people are known as the "hands" of the organization, and will see that any task is done, and are extremely and highly motivated individuals. People with the gift of ministry or the gift of service will many times over extend themselves and will become frustrated with their situation because they don't seem to have enough hours in the day to get everything done. They like short-term goals and expectations, so that they can move on to another area of need.

Spiritual Gifts Wrapped Up

> *For by one Spirit we were all baptized into one body—whether Jews or Greeks, whether slaves or free—and have all been made to drink into one Spirit. For in fact the body is not one member but many.*
>
> *1 Corinthians 12:13–14*

As you have learned through this overview of our spiritual gifts that our Heavenly Father has bestowed upon each and every human being, these gifts are for the benefit of us all. Just as no one individual is an island, neither is there a human being alive that will have each and every one of these spiritual gifts with the exception that Jesus had them all, because he was all man and all God. We need each other regardless of what spiritual gift our Heavenly Father has given us, so that we all are joined together to form ONE BODY. Just as a human body has many billions of cells that make up the entire body, each part of the body has many billions of cells that make up each individual member of that body. It requires every one of us to complete the entire body. Until we recognize that these gifts are not just for being used on Sundays and Wednesdays church services but are necessary for our daily lives and businesses in which we work, we will not become the built up and functioning body that Jesus was trying to teach us about in the scriptures.

> *As each one has received a gift, minister it to one another, as good stewards of the manifold grace of God. If anyone speaks, let him speak as the oracles of God. If anyone ministers, let him do it as with the ability which God supplies, that in all things God may be glorified through Jesus Christ, to who belong the glory and the dominion forever and ever. Amen.*
>
> 1 Peter 4:10–11

Dear Heavenly Father, I understand that I have gifts, talents and abilities hidden deep within me that you have deposited, and just as an apple tree doesn't struggle to produce apples, neither are the gifts that I have within me a struggle for me. Allow me to see and to recognize my gifts, talents and abilities as your gifts, and help me to use them, as you would have me to. In Jesus' name AMEN!

Death Issues

One of the major issues within the Christian faith today is how should we respond when a parent, or family member who has caused us so much pain, both physically, emotionally, and maybe even sexually, dies. Not that we really want to rejoice over their death, because somehow that seems wrong in our culture today, but should we be forced or made to feel guilty over the fact that we don't have any tears to shed over their death. Evil has many faces and in fact, many times those faces are those closest to us that are supposed to love and care for us. Through this chapter I hope to shed some light on this subject for others that may have experienced this same situation, and allow God's freedom to shine into your life through His Word regarding such a horrible situation. I am speaking from a point of view that I myself had to come to terms with just recently, and the Lord gave me His Peace that I now want to share with you on this subject.

In our lives and relationships with others, sometimes those situations require comfort and peace that only our Heavenly Father can give. When dealing with a biological family situation that involves any type of abuse, whether it is physical, emotional, or sexual in nature, many times the person that has had the trauma perpetrated on them of such abuses will feel that they have nowhere to turn when their abuser(s) dies. Adult survivors of childhood abuses many times have allowed themselves to bury the abuse within their minds, and have gone on with their lives as nothing has happened. Only when the perpetrator of those abuses dies, will the survivor of the abuses seem to digress into the realms of their traumatic experiences, and now they don't know how to deal with the issues of how to feel about the death of their abuser(s). Even if the survivor of abusive situations have forgiven the abuser(s), that doesn't mean that they have forgotten the trauma, or the emotional scars that such abuse leaves behind. Only God can truly give the peace and comfort that an abuse survivor needs.

The first thing that any survivor of abuse must do is to distance themselves from their abuser(s). As adults, this is a rather simple thing to do, since we can choose whom we have in our lives and whom we don't. However, even as adult survivors of abuse, the fact still remains that one day those who have harmed us, will eventually die, and what we survivors must do again is deal with our emotions and feelings over the death of the abuser(s), all over again. Somehow, as survivors, we become torn, between protecting ourselves from further harm, especially if one abuser(s) is still living and one has died, and family responsibilities and or preconceived ideas of family obligations and responsibilities. This can also rear its ugly head in situations where no one else in the family knows of the past abuses and without realizing it can perpetuate the abuse onto the survivor by not understanding why they are not engaging in the family obligations and responsibilities surrounding the loss of the abuser(s)/family member.

Let me first say, nowhere throughout the entire bible does it say anything about we are required to attend funerals, pay our condolences or even to receive condolences for the death of a family member. Period. With that being said, the question now becomes; how does an adult survivor of abuse handle this type of situation? On the one hand, if the survivor doesn't make a "showing" in remembrance of the abuser(s) they are seen as cold, cruel, or calloused. On the other hand, if the survivor of abuse does subject themselves to "honor" the death of the person, then they are bombarded with "What a good person they were," and "Oh, How they will be missed." These types of statements will only serve to send daggers of more pain into a survivor of abuse and send them into a tailspin of emotions because the people making "nice" about the dead person, when so much evil was done by them in their lifetime. Nowhere in the bible does it tell us that we aren't allowed to say what the person was really like while they were living. This is simply a matter of folklore and tradition handed down through the ages, that somehow we could only say nice things about the dead, regardless of how they lived out their life.

First, let's look at this one step at a time.

Realizing that you weren't to blame for the abuse

As a survivor of abuse many times the first hurdle that we must face is that we didn't cause this abusive situation to happen to us. Many times as survivors of childhood abuses, we feel that we somehow caused our abuser(s) to abuse us. This is simply a lie planted within the scope of the abusive situation, to render you helpless and hopeless. This has NEVER been your fault and NEVER will be your fault that the abuser(s) in your life chose to do you harm. Survivors of abuse must first come to terms that they didn't cause the abuse to happen to them, however NOW, they have a course of action to prevent the abuse from continuing.

Forgiveness

As a survivor of abuse committed by those that were supposed to love, care and protect you, this step is the hardest but most important step in the process of surviving the abuses from your past. Often times, we confuse forgiveness with condoning ones actions, and this is simply not the case. Even the bible tells us:

> *The memory of the righteous is blessed, But the name of the wicked will rot.*
>
> *Proverbs 10:7*

Jewish understanding of Proverbs 10:7 is that what this scripture is basically saying is; that that memory of a righteous person will be remembered with honor, and praise. Whereas when the name of a wicked person is mentioned, it will leave a bad taste in the mouth will leave ill feelings when that person's name is spoken, and will ultimately be forgotten and no longer mentioned. Forgiveness is required for anyone and especially a survivor to get past the offences done to them. Even Jesus spoke words of forgiveness over the very ones that were crucifying Him that day, and wasn't that the harshest form of abuse?

> *Then Jesus said, "Father forgive them, for they do not know what they do."*
>
> *Luke 23:34*

Jesus was able to ask that the Father forgive them in the middle of his abusive situation. Consider then how much more power we as Christians now hold, seeing that we have such an advocate with the Father in Jesus himself, who endured the harshest of situations of abuse that we could ever endure.

Forgiveness isn't vindicating the abuser(s), forgiveness is releasing you from their hold on you. To forgive your abuser(s) is to set yourself free from the abuser(s) grasp; however, that doesn't mean that you don't guard your heart and yourself from becoming entangled again in their abuses of you. When you forgive them their trespasses against you, you have actually become the person of power over that situation. Forgiveness is NOT a free ride over your life any longer; it is actually a free ticket into God's hands to handle the matter. When we refuse to forgive our abuser(s), we somehow think that we can pay them back for the pain that they have caused us, when in reality, God tells us in His Word:

> *Beloved, do not avenge yourselves, but rather give place to wrath; for it is written, "Vengeance is Mine, I will repay," says the Lord.*
>
> Romans 12:19

> *Vengeance is Mine, and recompense; Their foot shall slip in due time; For the day of their calamity is at hand, And the things to come hasten upon them.*
>
> Deuteronomy 32:35

Choice is yours

Now the choice is yours to decide whether to allow your abuser(s) close enough into your life to possibly harm you or someone close to you again. Just because you have forgiven them doesn't mean that you have now somehow become "brain dead" to the issues at hand. That they have abused you, you have forgiven them of their abuse of you, and now you must decide how much you are willing to allow them access into your life from this point on. When I talk about access to your life, I really mean into your heart and your everyday living. When we become close enough to other people in our life, we open ourselves up to the possibility to get hurt. This is simply a fact of life. However, as a survivor of abuse, we tend to be a little more cautious of whom we allow into our lives. However, this choice has pros and cons to it, and we will examine our options in this section.

Depending on your individual situation that you have survived, the choice may be an easy decision, or a more difficult decision. That is for you and you alone with God to decide how to proceed from here. However, as a survivor myself, and ministering to other survivors, I have developed some helpful thoughts to ponder as you are making your decision.

Has your abuser(s) stopped abusing others that they are in contact with or not?

In my years of ministering to survivors of abuse, and my personal experiences with this topic, I have found that this must be the first question that we need answered. Abuser(s) typically have a pattern to their abusive nature. If your abuser(s) was emotionally abusive, typically these abuser(s) don't stop abusing those that they come into contact with. This is a matter of their character of wanting to control and manipulate others around them. Emotional abuser(s) have the type personalities that they can tear other's emotions down and grind them into the dust, while other's that they are around can be built up and inspired by their charm and grace in any given situation. This is their way of controlling every situation and the people that they are exposed to, designed for one thing, what they desire from the relationship. In these types of abusive situations, I have found that the only way to deal with them is NOT to deal with them at all. They are sociopathic by their very nature, and will con their way into the very fabric of your soul each time you are in contact with them. Emotional abuse is one of the most evil forms of abuse because it doesn't leave scars or bruises on the outside, they are inward in their abusive damage. This abuser is commonly referred to as having the Spirit of Jezebel, and in order for this type of abuser(s) to continue they must have or create an Ahab (victim) to control and manipulate. Everyone that this type abuser(s) comes into contact with will become a victim to their enchanting means of manipulation and control. Emotional abuse fractures the soul of the survivor of this type of abuse, and often times goes the most unnoticed by others. Survivors of emotional abuse will many times display signs of distrust around their abuser(s) and possibly around strangers by becoming withdrawn, soft spoken, and will often act like they would rather wither away into the woodwork if it were possible.

Physical abuser(s) are different from emotional abuser(s) in that they want to see the pain that they have inflicted upon their chosen recipient. They want to know that they have inflicted some form of pain to their victims, and as such, are the abuser(s) that are most often noticed within our society today. Physical abuser(s) have a commonality with emotional abuser(s) in that they feel that by their physical abuse of a person they have demonstrated their power and superiority over their victims. It's still a control thing with them, however, their means of control is through violence and not manipulation of others emotions. When physical abuser(s) stop abusing, the abuse is stopped by receiving counseling/treatment for their violent behaviors towards others, or they have converted to emotional abuses against others. In these types of situations, a survivor must ascertain why the physical abuse has stopped. Did it stop because the abuser(s) received some sort of treatment for their violent behavior, or has there simply been a changed in the nature of their abusive tactics? Is there evidence proving that their physical abusiveness has stopped or is it wishful or hopeful thinking on your part?

Sexual abusers ARE SELDOM IF NEVER CURED, and will cannot stop their abuse, regardless of whether they have received treatment for their behavior or not. The only way that sexual abusers stop their abuses is by not having access to victims. This is why we have the Sex Offender Lists that these types of offenders must be registered on, to help protect the public. These types of abuser(s)s are mentally impaired by their addiction to the sexual nature of their abuse. The best advice is protect yourself and others from these types of abuser(s)s, by not allowing them an avenue for their abusive tendencies.

Depending on what your choice is, regarding the continued relationship with your abuser(s) will give you an insight as to what choice you make in determining how to handle the death of your abuser(s). Regardless of whether you have chosen to remove yourself from the life of your abuser(s) or to allow them to remain in your life, you are under no obligation in the Eyes of God as to how or what you decide when it comes to memorializing their death. You are under no obligation to subject yourself to any further emotional abuse by placing yourself in the middle of the hornet's nest of well-wishers and condolences for the loss of someone that caused you such pain. If you removed the abuser(s) from your life prior to their death, then the point that you removed them from your life long before they died also means that you in fact have already grieved for that loss (or maybe you haven't and you should allow yourself to). That also means that you have and have laid that issue aside and been healed through your forgiveness of their trespasses against you. Regardless of your decision, you should never buy into the guilt that others may try to place upon you during this time of the abuser(s) demise, regardless of who they are, nor how you are related to them. Forgive the emotional trappers for they don't know or understand what they are doing by trying to guilt you into something that you don't want to do, and enjoy your life, as you have. Dead is Dead and Life Goes On. Don't buy into the guilt that others are trying to control you with through this situation, knowing that not one mention from God and His Word ever condemned someone for not showing up at funeral. NOT ONCE!

Three Dimensions of Covenants

Your first question probably is "What is a Covenant?" The simple answer is that covenants are agreements between two or more parties, coming together for a common cause or goal. In this section, we will expand on that simple answer so that you have a clear understanding of what a covenant is and how covenants are a significant part of our everyday lives. Many times, we will enter into covenant agreements without ever having a clue that we have made covenant agreements that are binding, and many times, we should be treating them as legally and morally binding.

There are three dimensions of covenant agreements that we will explore throughout this section, and each carry with them some commonalities. All covenant agreements will have terms of agreements by one or both of the parties involved. All covenant agreements will be sealed with some form of acceptance by one or both of the parties involved. All covenant agreements will have terms for one or both of the parties to comply with and consequences for failing to comply with the terms and conditions of the agreement. Finally, all covenant agreements will fall into one of two categories, conditional or unconditional, meaning that either party will be bound to the conditions of the agreement or in the case of unconditional covenant agreements, one or all parties are not bound to any conditions for the covenant to remain enforce.

The three dimensions of covenant agreements is either an agreement between men with other men, which includes leaders of countries with other countries as in Peace Treaties, and trade agreements. Men with God, where often times men will make agreements with God regarding life situations, but God was not the originator of such covenant agreement, but will accept the persons willingness to try to keep such an agreement. An example of this type of covenant originating with Man are agreements that "I will not do this or that, if you God will do this or that thing for me", which as we know, and even God knows the heart of man, that man may or may not be able to live up to this type of agreement. The final dimension of a covenant agreement is God with Man where God is the originator of the covenant agreement, such as the case with the Ten Commandants given to Moses on Mount Sinai, God originated that covenant, and Man accepts them as an agreement between him and God.

Throughout our lives, we all have conditional and unconditional covenant agreements and we should begin to consider them more carefully. A prime example of covenant agreements that were broken and the consequences or impact that they had on ordinary people's lives were the contracts written and sold during the mortgage crisis in 2008. These home loans were covenant contracts between men that many times knew that the person whom they were making the contracts with were not going to be able to live up to the conditions described within the agreement, hence the housing crisis. We will begin this section exploring different covenant agreements within the three dimensions. This study will help us to understand each dimension, and their influences on our daily life.

The First Dimension of Covenant Agreements

Covenants Between Men

The first dimension of covenants is the covenants between men. Covenants between men come in many forms, and with many different intentions and conditions. All covenants between men are conditional covenants, and require that all parties involved to keep the covenant intact to carry out the performance. In this chapter, we will begin to explore what a covenant between men looks like and provide you with biblical examples. You will be gaining an everyday understanding on how we use these covenants without even realizing it.

Covenants between men include, treaties, alliance agreements, business contracts, and among friends, there are covenants whether written or unwritten. In each of these, a covenant agreement has been created and carries with them conditions that each party expects to take place within the agreement or covenant. Let's begin first by exploring treaties and alliance agreements. Treaties and alliance agreements are typically formed between countries for the purpose of trading goods, services, protection, and even when declaring war or peace with rival nations. There are always people behind these agreements, and that is why they are listed within the context of covenants between men. A prime example of a treaty or alliance agreement that is mired in so much controversy today, the Middle East Peace Treaty, between Israel and the Palestinian people. It is appropriately called the Land for Peace deal, which is just another term for a covenant agreement. In this covenant, the Palestinians want Israel to give up land in order to have peace within their borders. Notice, both parties have items that they must perform in order for the covenant to be accepted, and a covenant resolution made. An example of an alliance agreement is a contract between companies that agree to conduct business in conjunction with each other for the fulfillment of business projects and ventures. Such alliances are formed to help each organization involved control their costs of doing business, and will often times be limited in nature to a particular service, or product. A prime example of an alliance agreement is with your cellphone and the service providers. Have you ever noticed that many times certain phones are only available from certain providers? This is because of an alliance covenant agreement between two or more businesses. In the business world, a business is treated just like individuals and hence is the reason that this type of alliance agreement is still considered a covenant between men, the word men being neutral in gender.

Business contracts are considered covenant agreements between men because they stipulate monetary contributions in exchange for services rendered. A good example of a business contract is the mortgage on your home. The lender has agreed to lend you the money that you need in order to purchase your first home. The loan documents that you sign at the closing of the deal are considered a covenant agreement between you and the lender that you will repay the lender the money they provided for your home purchase, and have agreed to a particular interest rate in exchange for that loan. The agreement is limited to you paying off the agreement, and thereby dissolving or completing the covenant items contained within the contract. Another example of a business contract would be the contract that many sign in the corporate world. These contracts are covenant agreements between employers and employees, stating the amount of compensation the employee will receive for their services rendered as an employee. This too is a covenant agreement.

Lastly, friendships can be bound by covenant agreements that may or may not be written agreements. Consider if you will your closest friend. That friend expects that you will not betray their confidence, their character, or their integrity right? In return you expect that friend to not to betray you either, right? Can you see that this too is a covenant agreement even though neither one of you sat down, nor wrote out all the rules to your friendship? Another example of a covenant agreement between men, and the word men is gender neutral, is within the marriage of two people. Notice the words within the marriage ceremony, "to have and to hold from this day forward, so long as you both shall live." That is covenant language and it is conditional, which will be dissolved, upon the death of one of the two people being married.

Let's explore some biblical examples of this type of covenant agreements between men, and see that covenant agreements have been common to man throughout the ages. In 1 Samuel 18:3 we read that Jonathan and David made a covenant agreement between themselves because they loved each other and wanted that secure their friendship with a binding covenant agreement between themselves.

> *Then Jonathan and David made a covenant, because he loved him as his own soul. And Jonathan took off the robe that was on him and gave it to David, with his armor, even to his sword and his bow and his belt.*
>
> 1 Samuel 18:3 & 4

Notice that King David regarded the covenant agreement that he had with Jonathan as still in effect even to Jonathan's family. We see this is true when we read 2 Samuel where David having inquired if there were any still alive of Saul and Jonathan's family that he could show kindness too because of his covenant agreement that he had with Jonathan.

> *Now David said, "Is there still anyone who is left of the house of Saul, that I may show him kindness for Jonathan's sake?"*
>
> 2 Samuel 9:1

> *So David said to him, "Do not fear, for I will surely show you kindness for Jonathan your father's sake, and will restore to you all the land of Saul your grandfather; and you shall eat bread at my table continually."*
>
> 2 Samuel 9:7

Another family connection covenant can be found in: Genesis 31:50–52 in connection with Laban and Jacob. Throughout the Bible, we also have scriptural examples of covenants between men in gaining assistance during times of war and protection from harm. One such example is found in the book of 1 Kings.

> *Then Asa took all the silver and gold that was left in the treasuries of the house of the LORD and the treasuries of the king's house, and delivered them into the hand of his servants. And King Asa sent them to Ben-Hadad the son of Tabrimmon, the son of Hezion, king of Syria, who dwelt in Damascus, saying, "Let there be a treaty between you and me, as there was between my father and your father. See, I have sent you a present of silver and gold. Come and break your treaty with Baasha king of Israel, so that he will withdraw from me."*
>
> *1 Kings 15:18 & 19*

We will deal with the details of this covenant agreement that Asa made that day in another book; we just wanted you to see that covenants, treaties, etc… have been a part of man's life since God created the world. Some covenants can be for our benefit, and some covenants as we will see later, can actually be to our detriment.

Another example of a covenant agreement providing protection or aid can be seen in:

> *But they said, "We have certainly seen that the LORD is with you. So we said, 'Let there now be an oath between us, between you and us; and let us make a covenant with you, that you will do us no harm, since we have not touched you, and since we have done nothing to you but good and have sent you away in peace. You are now the blessed of the LORD.'"*
>
> *Genesis 26:28 &29*

Other examples of covenant agreements between men securing trade agreements, land agreements, and peace agreements can be found in the following scriptures:

Genesis 23:14–16, Joshua 9:15 & 16, and 1 Kings 5:5–11.

As you can see, covenant agreements are in integral part of our daily lives whether we choose to acknowledge them or not. We need to understand how covenants work within the framework of our everyday lives so that we can begin to become more responsible in our agreements and our conduct among ourselves as a society. One look into the gangs and mobs and anyone can see that they boil down to covenant agreements. These are examples of wrongly placed covenant agreements however; they are covenant agreements and carry consequences for failure to abide by certain provisions within those groups and agreements.

> *Heavenly Father, help me to recognize that every agreement that I make is a covenant agreement in your eyes. And father please help me to know when I shouldn't be making such a covenant agreement in a particular situation, because it is not a health agreement to be made. I only want pure and wholesome covenant agreement between me and my fellow man, and only with your help, can I avoid the wrongly placed agreements. In Jesus' name AMEN!*

The Second Dimension of Covenant Agreements

Men with God

We have heard it said many times throughout our lives, "Not make a vow to God that you can't keep." However, how many of us really understand that a vow is a covenant agreement? That is exactly what that statement means, don't make a Covenant Agreement with God that you can't keep. In this chapter, we are going to look at several instances throughout the bible of vows or covenant agreements that men and women made to God, and we will soon learn the importance of making and keeping our covenant agreements or vows. Let us first start with the scripture in Proverbs.

> *It is a snare for a man to devote rashly something as holy, And afterward to reconsider his vows.*
>
> *Proverbs 20:25*

How many times have we heard of people who get themselves or find themselves in awkward or even dangerous situations, and cry out a vow to God to save them from this or that. They vow that they will do such and so for Him for the rest of their lives, only to act as if they had never made a promise or vow once they are out of harm's way. This is exactly what this scripture is talking about. Never should we hastily utter a vow or covenant agreement that only seeks to get us out of a bind now. This is a trap or a snare to your own soul when you hastily proclaim a vow to God if He will protect or remove you from the situation that you find yourself in. Covenant agreements or vows are serious business with God, and as a matter of fact, the entire bible of God's word is based upon a covenant agreement, however we will be getting more into that in the next chapter. For now, let's look at some examples of rash or hastily proclaimed vows, and their results.

> Then the Spirit of the LORD came upon Jephthah, and he passed through Gilead and Manasseh, and passed through Mizpah of Gilead; and from Mizpah of Gilead he advanced toward the people of Ammon. And Jephthah made a vow to the LORD, and said, "If You will indeed deliver the people of Ammon into my hands, then it will be that whatever comes out of the doors of my house to meet me, when I return in peace from the people of Ammon, shall surely be the LORD's, and I will offer it up as a burnt offering."
>
> So Jephthah advanced toward the people of Ammon to fight against them, and the LORD delivered them into his hands. And he defeated them from Aroer as far as Minnith—twenty cities—and to Abel Keramim, with a very great slaughter. Thus the people of Ammon were subdued before the children of Israel.
>
> When Jephthah came to his house a Mizpah, there was his daughter, coming out to meet him with timbrels and dancing; and she was his only child. Besides her he had neither son nor daughter. And it came to pass,

when he saw her that he tore his clothes, and said, "Alas, my daughter! You have brought me very low! You are among those who trouble me! For I have given my word to the LORD, and I cannot go back on it."

Judges 12:29–35

Now, in the previous verse of scriptures we see a man, a judge over Israel, had the Spirit of the Lord with him in his endeavors, however, he rashly made a vow or covenant to insure that his success would continue. This vow was at a GREAT cost to himself since what he vowed as offered unto the Lord was his only daughter. One wonders why a person having success in his previous battles would offer up his child. Could it be that he felt that he had gained all his previous victories by only his own hand, that God didn't have anything to do with it? Certainly seems to be the case, since he was asking the Lord for something that was already upon him according to the first sentence in this verse of scripture. Isn't that the same thing we are sometimes guilty of in our lives, when we think that our victories are by our own doing, and do not have anything to do with God? This is what is known as; a rash or a hastily conceived covenant agreement done without thoughtful consideration, and what the scripture in Proverbs warns us about. Not only did Jephthah make this rash vow to the Lord, when he determined what it was going to cost him, he began scolding his daughter for being one of those that troubles him. She didn't have anything to do with the vow he so hastily vowed in the heat of wanting victory at any cost. This is what happens when vows and covenant agreement are entered into so lightly or flippantly, there are consequences to be paid, and others might be hurt unintentionally by our commitments made.

Let's now go into the New Testament of the bible and see another example of a vow or covenant agreement that was hastily conceived, and the price that was paid.

> *Now the multitude of those who believed were of one heart and one soul; neither did anyone say that any of the things he possessed was his own, but they had all things in common.*
>
> Acts 4:32

Notice that this congregation obviously had a covenant agreement among themselves, seeing that they all agreed that their possessions were all common to the group so that none said that anything that was owned was their own. According to background research, this congregation had agreed among themselves that possessors of lands and houses would sell them and bring the full amount into the congregation to be distributed to any who came with a need. Scripture doesn't tell us whether or not they were required to sell their property, just that since the covenant agreement between the members of the congregation had established that as the property was sold the full amount of the proceeds were for the benefit of expanding the gospel to be distributed by the apostles. Now here comes the following situation:

> *But a certain man name Ananias, with Sapphira his wife, sold a possession. And he kept back part of the proceeds, his wife also being aware of it, and brought a certain part and laid it at the apostles' feet.*
>
> Acts 5:1–2

Ananias along with his wife Sapphira having sold property and conspired between themselves that they would only give a portion of the proceeds and keep a portion of the proceeds for themselves. They compounded their deception by pretending to lay the entire payment at the feet of the apostle's when in fact it was only a portion of the proceeds.

> *But Peter said, "Ananias, why has Satan filled your heart to lie to the Holy Spirit and keep back part of the price of the land for yourself? While it remained, was it not your own? And after it was sold, was it not in your own control? Why have you conceived this thing in your heart? You have not lied to men but to God."*
>
> Acts 5:3–4

> *Then Ananias hearing these words, fell down and breathed his last. So great fear came upon all those who heard these things.*
>
> Acts 5:5

> *Now it was about three hours later when his wife came in, not knowing what had happened. And Peter answered her, "Tell me whether you sold the land for so much?"*
> *She said, "Yes, for so much."*
>
> Acts 5:7–8

> *Then immediately she fell down at his feet and breathed her last. And the young men came in and found her dead, and carrying her out, buried her by her husband.*
>
> Acts 5:10

The fact that Ananias had made the covenant agreement with the group to God that they held all things in common Ananias and his wife were not completely sold out or committed to the agreement that was made. They conspired together to only pretend to have given the entire proceeds so that no man of the group would know that they withheld a portion for themselves. However, the Holy Spirit being active within the group, and being a witness to the covenant agreement knew what they had done, and an example for that congregation and for us needed to be made on the seriousness of our covenant agreements that we make especially those that we make to God. Then end result for Ananias and Sapphira was immediate death. It is a common understanding that Ananias and Sapphira only wanted to appear righteous to the group, when in fact their hearts were not committed to what their mouth and actions confessed. Another point that we could make here is that since Ananias' wife didn't know what had just happened to her husband, a few hours prior, she could have confessed that the amount that Peter asked her about was only a portion of the sale and not the full amount. Based upon what Peter had inquired of her that day, her life would have been spared and she would have been held in high regards within the group for not trying to continue the deception that she and her husband had conspired against the group and God. We could also see that by Peter's question, that the Holy Spirit might have exalted her for her forthrightness, instead of removing her last breath for lying to Him and the group to only appear to be committed. This also makes the case for having more reverential fear of the Holy Spirit and of God, than you have for how you appear before men.

Other examples of covenant agreements that people have made with God are given for examples to us, and with further study, we will learn the seriousness of making covenant agreements or vows to God. True and pure covenant agreements or vows with God should always be connected to His promises so as to avoid the mistakes that we saw others make in the rash or hastily conceived vows or agreements. *If you don't know His promises, then don't make the covenant!* The first example we will look at is the covenant that Jacob made with God.

> *Then Jacob made a vow, saying, "If God will be with me, and keep me in this way that I am going, and give me bread to eat and clothing to put on, so that I come back to my father's house in peace, then the LORD shall be my God. And this stone which I have set as a pillar shall be God's House, and of all that You give me I will surely give a tenth to You."*
>
> *Genesis 28:20–22*

Some background on Jacob's vow is at the beginning of this chapter in the bible, his father Isaac blessed him with a father's blessing that God would bless him, and makes him fruitful and multiply him so that he became a great assembly of people, and inherited the land that God gave to their father Abraham for him to possess. On this blessing, Jacob set out to obtain a wife from the daughters of Laban, his mother's brother. While on his way, he made camp one night without his knowledge, at the very place where God had appeared to Abraham, many years prior. As Jacob slept, he had a vision of what is known as Jacob's ladder, with the angels of God ascending and descending on it. When Jacob woke from his sleep, he was awe-struck to realize that

God was truly in this place, and named this place Bethel, meaning the House of God. The Spirit of the Lord had visited and confirmed his covenant agreement to him that he had with Abraham and Isaac. God confirmed that he would indeed give him and his descendants the land on which he had slept. This also confirmed the blessing that Isaac had pronounced over him prior to his departure, to give him the choice to make a conditional covenant agreement to God that he would give God a tenth of all that God would provide for him. Notice that Jacob made this vow or covenant agreement based upon promises already given to him twice, once by his father Isaac, and again from God himself. Notice that God didn't require the covenant that Jacob made, however Jacob was so overcome with awe that the Lord was truly in that place where he was, that he wanted of his own free will, establish a covenant agreement with the God of his fathers. Therefore, we should consider the example that Jacob has given us and any covenant agreements that we might make with God.

When we titled this chapter Covenants that Men make with God, the word men is gender neutral. Both a man or woman is free to make a covenant agreement with God, of his or her own free will, and that has and will not ever change. However, anyone that chooses to make a covenant agreement with the Lord should prayerfully and mindfully consider what they are dedicating to the Lord as their part of the covenant agreement, and as we have discussed, we should be certain that we have a promise of God to base any covenant that we make. Such is the next example that we will look at that was made by Hannah.

> *Then she made a vow and said, "O LORD of hosts, if You will indeed look on the affliction of Your maidservant*

and remember me, and not forget Your maidservant, but will give Your maidservant a male child, then I will give him to the LORD all the days of this life, and no razor shall come upon his head."

1 Samuel 1:11

Hannah, being a wife of a devoted man, serving the Lord faithfully year after year, Hannah was basing her covenant agreement with the Lord upon a promise that the Lord had given to all who were obedient to His word as we see in what is known as the fifth book of Moses:

"Then it shall come to pass, because you listen to these judgments, and keep and do them, that the LORD your God will keep with you the covenant and the mercy which He swore to your father. And He will love you and bless you and multiply you; He will also bless the fruit of your womb and the fruit of your land, your grain and your new wine and your oil, the increase of your cattle and the offspring of your flock, in the land of which He swore to your fathers to give you. You shall be blessed above all people; there shall not be a male or female barren among you or among your livestock. And The LORD will take away from you all sickness, and will afflict you with none of the terrible diseases of Egypt which you have known, but will lay them on all those who hate you."

Deuteronomy 7:12–15

As you can see, covenant agreements of men or women with God have occurred throughout time, however, we would do well to heed the examples given to us in the scriptures on the seriousness of such agreements. We must be prepared to fulfill our part of any covenant agreement that we might make with the Lord, knowing that He will fulfill His part. Furthermore, we should ascertain first what God's Word has to say regarding any covenant agreement that we would seek to make, and more importantly:

> *If you don't know His promises, then don't make the covenant!*

Heavenly Father, I only want to make covenant agreements with you based upon your promises that I have found and taken into my heart through your Word. Help me to locate your promises within your Word so that I have a correct base upon which to make any covenant agreement that I might make with you. In Jesus' name AMEN!

The Third and Ultimate Dimension of Covenant Agreements

God With Man

The third and ultimate covenant agreement is the covenant established by God with each of us. It is our choice to enter into it or not, but it is a covenant agreement nonetheless. As we examine how this covenant agreement came into being, we will further understand how and why this is the ultimate dimension of Covenant Agreements. As we have learned in the previous chapters on the three dimensions of covenant agreements, we saw that all covenant agreements have the same characteristics in common:

1. They are entered into voluntarily
2. They can be conditional or unconditional
3. They all have witnesses
4. All Covenant Agreements have some type of seal or sign to them

The last dimension of covenant agreements draws us to the final and ultimate covenant agreement that God made with man. The purpose of understanding the previous dimensions of covenant agreements brings us a clearer understanding to the ultimate dimension of the covenant agreement that God had plan all along. Had we not been given the previous examples of covenant agreements then we wouldn't fully understand or grasp the importance to this final covenant agreement. Nor would we understand the complexities of God's reasoning for providing His only begotten Son as He did. Almost everyone has heard and knows the scripture,

> *For God so loved the world that He gave His only begotten Son, that whoever believes in Him should not perish but have everlasting life. For God did not send His Son into the world to condemn the world, but that the world through Him might be saved.*
>
> John 3:16–17

However, how many of us realized that this is actually a Covenant Agreement that God was making with humankind? This is exactly why we need to fully grasp the understanding of covenant agreements and to rest in the assurance that God bound himself into a covenant agreement with each of us, but offering us His Son's blood as the sealing or binding force of this agreement. Through that precious blood of Jesus, we enter into a blood-sworn covenant with God.

Through the following scriptures, we will see the meticulous and powerful work that Jesus provided for each of us on that cross and through His resurrection three days later.

Jesus was the central part to the Covenant, without His sacrifice, there would have been no covenant agreement.

> *"I the LORD, have called You in righteousness, And will hold Your hand; I will keep You and give You as a covenant to the people, As a light to the Gentiles, To open blind eyes, To bring out prisoners from the prison, Those who sit in darkness from the prison house.*
>
> Isaiah 42:6 & 7

Jesus is the facilitator of the Covenant between God and man in this Ultimate Covenant agreement.

> *But now He has obtained a more excellent ministry, inasmuch as He is also Mediator of a better covenant, which was established on better promises. For if that first covenant had ben faultless, then no place would have been sought for a second. Because finding fault with them, He says: "Behold, the days are coming says the LORD, when I will make a new covenant with the house of Israel and with the house of Judah—not according to the covenant that I made with their fathers in the day when I took them by the hand to lead them out of the land of Egypt; because they did not continue in My covenant, and I disregarded them, says the LORD.*
>
> Hebrews 8:6–9

> *Not with the blood of goats and calves, but with His own blood He entered the Most Holy Place once for all, having obtained eternal redemption. how much more shall the blood of Christ, who through the eternal Spirit offered Himself with spot to God, cleanse your conscience from dead works to serve the living God? And for this reason He is the Mediator of the new covenant, by means of death, for the redemption of the transgressions*

> under the first covenant, that those who are called may receive the promise of eternal inheritance.
>
> Hebrews 9:12, 14 & 15

We see that Jesus provided the Best and Better covenant between God and man that is founded upon better promises. As we examine the previous covenants that God made with man in the Old Testament, they were and still are all pointing to the New and Better Covenant that Jesus provided for each of us. Understanding and examining the old covenant agreements sheds a brighter light of the strength and promises of the New Covenant. Furthermore, as we have seen where the covenant agreement between God and Man in the old covenant was renewed with each generation, Jesus was the final renewal of the covenant agreements that God originally had with the father's faith throughout the Old Testament of the bible.

In Genesis Chapter 15 and Genesis Chapter 17, we see the covenant agreement that God made with Abraham, God renewed the covenant agreement He had with Abraham with his son Isaac in Genesis chapter 17 and Genesis chapter 26. Then He renewed the covenant agreement with Jacob in Genesis chapter 28 and 1 Chronicles 16. Then renewed it again with David in 2 Samuel 23, and Psalms 89, and we are reminded of this covenant agreement in the New Testament. God was making the point like we many times will do with our own natural children by telling them, and telling them again, and telling them again, so that finally they might get it that He was making an UNBREAKABLE covenant agreement. JESUS IS THE FINAL & ULTIMATE DIMENSION OF THAT COVENANT AGREEMENT!

To perform the mercy promised to our fathers And to remember His holy covenant, The oath which He swore to our father Abraham: To grant us that we, Being delivered from the hand of our enemies, Might serve Him without fear, In holiness and righteousness before Him all the days of our life.

Luke 1:72–75

Yes, and all the prophets, from Samuel and those who follow, as many as have spoken, have also foretold these days. You are sons of the prophets, and of the covenant which God mad with our fathers, saying to Abraham, 'And in your seed all the families of the earth shall be blessed.' To you first, God, having raised up His Servant Jesus, sent Him to bless you, in turning away every one of you from your iniquities."

Acts 3:24–26

Dear Heavenly Father, bind this understanding of your ultimate covenant to my heart and cause me to know and understand the length, breath, and height of your love and care that you have for me to make such a covenant agreement with me. In Jesus', name AMEN!

Covenant Devotional Standing on the Promises of God

Back in the middle 80's when I came into the faith, the charismatic's of that time came out with a new "fad" idea that has stuck with me for all these years. That "fad" was called; The Promise Box; containing 365 scriptures written on little cards that you pulled one out each morning with your coffee. These are a wonderful way to begin getting The Word of God into you, however, if you don't ponder, study, and pray out each verse of scripture, you are only feeding on the MILK of the Word, and as with everything, God's Word has so much more to feed your Spirit. You can still find them in most Christian bookstores to this day. However, I have done my "promise boxes" a little different. See, I believe that in order for God's promises to become second nature to our daily habits, those scripture promises must be REAL to each individual person, not just simply memorizing passages of scripture. If you never really sink your teeth into the meat or Covenant Promise that God has already made with each of us individually through the scriptures, we can never reach the heights of HIS KINGDOM way of life that Jesus died and rose again to obtain our access to ALL THE PROMISES and THE COVENANT.

Behaviorists tell us that it takes approximately 25 days to create a new habit. I believe that it takes the same amount of time to dwell and ponder on our Covenant Promise written by God in order for those promises to become something REAL and TANGIBLE for us to hold onto. When life changing events happen in our lives, and they do for all of us at different times in our lives, if we haven't planted, pondered, decreed, and declared the specific covenant promises that God has given us in HIS WORD, we will fail to achieve our HIGHEST NATURE, which is that same nature of God that Jesus has.

The following is a 12-month journey to your Personal and Spiritual development and enlightenment of the True Nature of God. Each month has a new Covenant Promises for you to ponder, pray and take as your own Covenant Promise. Each Covenant Promise has three different passages of scripture for you to proclaim and get down into your Spirit. The Word of God tells us that a three strand cord isn't easily broken, *Ecclesiastes 4:12* and those three different passages are the building blocks to your "LIFE CORD" which are GOD'S COVENANT PROMISES! I have provided a beginning prayer for each month's Covenant Promises to demonstrate how to begin praying to Our Father God and applying HIS words of LIFE to your own life and allowing God's Covenant Promise come alive in your Spirit. As you progress in feeding your Spirit, you will begin to change your prayer over the promises of God in order to fit your specific needs. I have provided an area for you to write your notes and adjust your prayers for those specific needs. I believe that it is truly important to keep some type of Prayer Journal, so that you can SEE over the course of time how God has answered every one of them.

January—Covenant of Peace

*And the L*ORD *spoke to Moses, saying: "Speak to Aaron and his sons, saying 'This is the way you shall bless the children of Israel. Say to them:*
*"The L*ORD *bless you and keep you;*
*The L*ORD *make His face shine upon you,*
And be gracious to you;
*The L*ORD *lift up His countenance upon you,*
And give you peace."
"So they shall put My name on the children of Israel, and I will bless them."

Numbers 6:22–27

Peace I leave with you, My pease I give to you; not as the world gives do I give to you. Let not your heart be troubled, neither let it be afraid.

John 14:27

Grace and peace be multiplied to you in the knowledge of God and of Jesus our Lord, as His divine power has given to us all things that pertain to life and godliness, through the knowledge of Him who called us by glory and virtue, by which have been given to us exceedingly great and precious promises, that through these you may be partakers of the divine nature, having escaped the corruption that is in the world through lust.

2 Peter 1:2–4

Dear Heavenly Father, your word tells me to remind you of your word not that your have forgotten, but to let you know that your WORD is truly a LIFE CORD or divine thread through the Life of your Son Jesus to mine. Your Word tells me that we are kings and priests just as Aaron was when Moses spoke your Words of Blessing over Aaron and his sons who were priests at the time. I am applying this Covenant of Peace to my life asking to bless and keep me throughout this day and every day that I wake. I thank you Lord that your face continually shines upon me as my banner of Peace over my life. Just as Jesus had that Covenant of Peace as His banner, so do I apply that same banner of Peace over my life and that Peace that surpasses all understanding will flow out to others throughout my day so that I am a carrier of that PEACE. Jesus himself gave this Covenant Banner of Peace to me, when he spoke those words to his disciples. I am a disciple of Christ, and apply His spoken promise of Peace so that my heart will NOT be troubled by what is going on around me. All is well with my soul because of this Covenant of Peace that is and was upon HIM and now is applied to my life. AMEN!

February—Covenant of Love

Jesus said to him, "'You shall love the L*ORD* *your God with all you heart, with all your soul, and with all your mind.' And the second is like it; 'You shall love your neighbor as yourself.' On these two commandments hang all the Law and the Prophets.*

Matthew 22:37–40

For I am persuaded that neither death nor life, nor angels nor principalities nor powers, nor thing present not things to come, nor height nor depth, nor any other created thing, shall be able to separate us from the love of God which is in Christ Jesus our Lord.

Romans 8:38–39

Just as He chose us in Him before the foundation of the world, that we should be holy and without blame before Him in Love having predestined us to adoption as sons by Jesus Christ to Himself, according to the good pleasure of His will.

Ephesians 1:4-5

Dear Heavenly Father, your word tells me to remind you of your word not that your have forgotten, but to let you know that your WORD is truly a LIFE CORD or divine thread through the Life of your Son Jesus to mine. Jesus instructed his disciples that the Greatest commandment that you have given us is that I am to love you GOD with all my heart and mind and soul and that I am to love others as I do myself. I am truly persuaded as the Apostle Paul is that NO THING can separate me from your LOVE that you gave when you gave your only begotten Son, Jesus, to rescue me from my unlovely ways. Thank you Father that you chose me through your Son Jesus before the foundation of the world was laid. I thank you Father that your Love is unconditional and never ending toward me and all your children. As I accept the Love that you are and apply your love to my life, I have that same unconditional love that I share as I go throughout my day and through that LOVE you have given you hold me blameless when I don't quite get that message across to others. Amen!

March—Covenant of Wisdom

O LORD, how manifold are Your works!
In wisdom You have made them all.
The earth is full of Your possessions—

Psalm 104:24

For the LORD give wisdom;
From His mouth come knowledge and understanding;
He stores up sound wisdom for the upright;
He is a shield to those who walk uprightly;

Proverbs 2:6–7

If any of you lacks wisdom, let him ask of God, who gives to all liberally and without reproach, and it will be given to him. But let him ask in faith, with no doubting, for he who doubts is like a wave of the sea driven and tossed by the wind.

James 1:5–6

Father, you say in your Word that if anyone lacks wisdom, we can freely ask and receive that wonder-working wisdom that created the world. Father open my eyes to see each day what your wisdom created because the earth is FULL of your wisdom made creations. I will listen for your wisdom that proceeds from your mouth and will allow it to seep deep into my Spirit so that I can walk each day with your wisdom and guidance, and with all your wisdom that you give I thank you that knowledge and understand comes with that wisdom. Amen!

April — Covenant of Grace

And of His fullness we have all received, and grace for grace.

John 1:16

You did not choose Me, but I chose you and appointed you that you should go and bear fruit and that your fruite should remain, that whatever you ask the Father in My name He may give you.

John 15:16

For it is God who works in you both to will and to do for His good pleasure.

Philippians 2:13

Thank you Father for I know that according to your Word you chose me and ordained me to go forth and bear fruit on this earth. Your word also tells me that if I ask anything in Jesus' name that it is your good pleasure and will to provide the Grace that I need at that time to walk through whatever may come my way this day. Amen!

May — Covenant of Strength

Wisdom and knowledge will be the stability of your times,
And the strength of salvation;
The fear of the LORD is His treasure.

Isaiah 33:6

But those who wait on the LORD
Shall renew their strength;
The shall mount up with wings like eagles,
The shall run and not be weary,
The shall walk and not faint.

Isaiah 40:31

Fear not, for I am with you;
Be not dismayed, for I am your God.
I will strengthen you,
Yes, I will help you,
I will uphold you with my righteous right hand.

Isaiah 41:10

Allow me to input a personal testimony around this verse of scripture, Isaiah 41:10. One of my daughters' had called to tell us that the doctors had found something that they wanted to remove. This was when she was 3 to 4 months pregnant with our granddaughter. Removing the questionable growth on her could possibly cause her to lose the baby. I told her, give me 5 minutes and I will call you back after I have heard how we are to pray over this situation. Two minutes later, I called her back and read this scripture over her that the Lord and given me. She went to the doctor for the procedure a couple of days later, they prepped her for the procedure, and suddenly the doctor said, "let's get one more look at this before we proceed." He and another doctor came back in the room from having done another sonogram, and said, "Get up, get dressed and go home, there is nothing there. We don't understand it, but we aren't going to do this procedure." PRAISE THE LORD! Our daughter and granddaughter were upheld by his Righteous Right Arm…just as he had told me!!!

> *Dear Heavenly Father, I thank you that you give me the wisdom, knowledge and understanding to wake and walk each day in. I know that daily you are upholding me with the strength of your righteous right hand, and I have nothing to fear each day because you are with me continually as I go throughout my day. I will walk and not faint, I will run and not get weary, and that by your strength I am able to rise above all situations that come my way today. AMEN!*

June—Covenant of Divine Health and Healing

Why are you cast down, O my soul?
And why are you disquieted within me?
Hope in God;
For I shall yet praise Him,
The help of my countenance and my God.

Psalm 43:5

Yes, we had the sentence of death in ourselves, that we should not rust in ourselves but in God who raises the dead, who delivered us from so great a death, and does deliver us; in whom we trust that He will still deliver us.

2 Corinthians 1:9–10

Beloved, I pray that you may prosper in all things and be in health, just as your soul prospers.

3 John 2

Father, I thank you that my health is evident upon the smile of my face, and know that whatever is disrupting my soul, you will calm. You, the Creator of all that is good and perfect, that raises the dead and delivers me daily from the taunts and torments of the enemy, that tries to make me forget your word of health and healing. I know that you shall deliver me from all the taunts and torments of the enemy, because above all you want that I should prosper and be in good health even as my soul prospers. AMEN!

July—Covenant of Blessing and Prosperity

May the Lord *God of your fathers make you a thousand times more numerous than you are, and bless you as He has promised you!*

Deuteronomy 1:11

When you eat the labor of your hands, You shall be happy, and it shall be well with you!

Psalm 128:2

And my God shall supply all your need according to His riches in glory by Christ Jesus.

Philippians 4:19

Father, I thank you that your word promises me that you will bless me and make me to be thousand times more than I already am. I thank you Father, that I am able to eat from the labor that you have provided for me to do, and that I am happy and fulfilled by all your goodness and mercy that surrounds me. In addition to all your blessings that you give me on daily basis I also thank you Father that whatever my needs for today might be, I know that you supply them through your Son, Jesus. Amen.

August—Covenant of Revelation and Understanding

And suddenly a voice came from heaven, saying, "This is My beloved Son, in whom I am well pleased."

Matthew 3:17

In whom are hidden all the treasures of wisdom and knowledge.

Colossians 2:3

Then He said to them, "These are the words which I spoke to you while I was still with you, that all things must be fulfilled which were written in the Law of Moses and the Prophets and the Psalms concerning Me." And He opened their understanding, that they might comprehend the Scriptures.

Luke 24:44–45

Dear Heavenly Father, your Son, Jesus has taught me to pray in His name because everything that I need each day come in and through HIM. All wisdom, knowledge and understanding come through Jesus, because I believe upon HIM as your Son. Through your Son Jesus, he has opened my understanding of all the words that you have written to me in your love letter called My Bible. Amen.

September—Covenant of Power

I indeed baptize you with water unto repentance, but He who is coming after me is mightier than I, whose sandals I am not worthy to carry. He will baptize you with the Holy Spirit and fire.

Matthew 3:11

And these signs will follow those who believe: In My name they will cast out demons; they will speak with new tongues; they will take up serpents; and if the drink anything deadly, it will by no means hurt them; they will lay hands on the sick, and they will recover."

Mark 16:17–20

And He said to them, "It is not for you to know times or seasons which the Father has put in His own authority. But you shall receive power when the Holy Spirit has come upon you; and you shall be witnesses to Me in Jerusalem, and in all Judea and Samaria, and to the end of the earth."

Acts 1:7–8

Dear Father, I have been baptized in water, accepted your Son Jesus as my Lord and Saviour and I ask that you baptize me with the Holy Ghost and fire. I understand the purpose of being baptized with your Holy Spirit is so that I will be a witness of Jesus wherever I may go. I further understand that, as a believer in the name of Jesus, your word says, that I shall lay hands on the sick and they SHALL recover, I will speak with a new tongue and show forth your marvelous working power all through the mighty name of Jesus. AMEN!

October — Covenant of Prayers Heard

"Most assuredly, I say to you, he who believe in Me, the works that I do he will do also; and greater works than these he will do, because I go to My Father. And whatever you ask in My name, that I will do, that the Father may be glorified in the Son. If you ask anything in My name, I will do it."

John 14:12–14

And in that day you will ask Me nothing. Most assuredly, I say to you, whatever you ask the Father in My name He will give you. Until now you have asked nothing in My name. Ask, and you will receive, that your joy may be full.

John 16:23–24

Now this is the confidence that we have in Him, that if we ask anything according to His will, He hears us. And if we know that He hears us, whatever we ask, we know that we have the petitions that we have asked of Him.

1 John 5:14–15

Thank you Father that you hear my prayers and my pleas. I know because your Word tells me that I can relax knowing that you will answer my prayers and pleas according to your time, and not mine. I am fully persuaded, that you hear and will answer my prayers so that my joy is full through Jesus and what he has done for me. AMEN!

November — Covenant of a New Heart

The poor shall eat and be satisfied;
Those who seek Him will praise the L̲ᴏʀᴅ.
Let your heart live forever!

Psalm 22:26

Then I will give them one heart, and I will put a new spirit within them, and take the stony heart out of their flesh, and give them a heart of flesh,

Ezekiel 11:19

I will give you a new heart and put a new spirit within you; I will take the heart of stone out of your flesh and give you a heart of flesh.

Ezekiel 36:26

Father, I ask you for that New Heart your promise in your Word. A heart that has your hopes and desires for my life and your desires that I should fulfill each and every day that I walk this earth. AMEN.

December—Covenant of Boldness

And when they had prayed, the place where they were assembled together was shaken; and they were all filled with the Holy Spirit, and they spoke the word of God with boldness.

Acts 4:31

in whom we have boldness and access with confidence through faith in Him.

Ephesians 3:12

"This is the covenant that I will make with than after those days, says the LORD: I will put My laws into their hearts, and in their minds I will write them," the He adds, "Their sins and their lawless deeds I will remember no more." Now where there is remission of these, there is no longer an offering for sin.

Therefore, brethren, having boldness to enter the Holiest by the blood of Jesus, by a new and living way which He consecrated for us, through the veil, that is His flesh, and having a High Priest over the house of God, let us draw near with a true heart in full assurance of faith, having our hearts sprinkled from an evil conscience and our bodies washed with pure water.

Hebrews 10:16:22

Thank you Father for the boldness to proclaim Jesus to all that I encounter each day. To be that living epistle read of all men because you have written your laws onto my heart that I am a disciple of Jesus and carry not only Him inside my Spirit, but also you, The Fullness of God. I have the boldness of a Lion, and am harmless as a dove to those around me because I have this confidence through Your Son Jesus. Thank you Father for giving me that same boldness that Jesus has. AMEN!

Keeping it Real

Throughout this book, we have discussed and laid out for you the basis for the nine basic elements of the Christian faith. In the final four chapters, we introduced you to the element that ties up the complete Christian belief system into the perfect and incorruptible Word of God. With every chapter throughout the book, we have given you the tools that you need to share your faith effectively throughout your daily life. With this final wrap up, I want to insure that you keep your faith real, alive, and relevant to this and future generations.

All too often, Christians are many times what I call "Pendulum Christians", they swing way too far to the left and then they swing way too far to the right, like that of a swinging pendulum. When this happens, many times, as the pendulum blade swings, unbelievers and new believers alike get sliced to shreds underneath their swinging blades of judgment and exuberance of their faith, and unbelievers and new Christians alike will decide that it isn't worth the trouble or effort to try and understand the Christian perspective. What I have tried to accomplish within a concisely written handbook is to show you a better way to sharing your faith with others and more effectively explaining just how simple becoming and remaining in the walk of a Christian life can really be.

As you continue with your bible study on your own, I would ask you to begin looking at the ordinary lives to the people that you will meet throughout the bible. God placed them there for us to know and understand, and He chose ordinary people to become His Extraordinary Saints. Prior to God entering their lives, they were just people like you and I, going through their daily lives. Once they accepted Jesus into their lives, their lives took on a much fuller dimension that what they had been experiencing. Look at the disciples that Jesus called first, they were fishermen fishing the sea for their livelihood, and notice that Jesus didn't take them away from their love, He expanded their love and passion to become fishers of men! They still were fishermen, however, Jesus just cast them into a fuller dimension of their passion, and He will do the same for whosoever will.

Jesus kept it real for everyone that He came into contact with, and if you are to follow the steps of Jesus, you too will need to Keep It Real with those around you. Share your faith; follow the chapters, only share what is REAL to you and your faith. As you do, you will be surprised to find just how many people will begin following you as you follow Christ throughout your life. You can live on someone else's revelation, just like you can live someone else's life, you have to live what is REAL to you, and others can only live what is REAL to them. Keep It REAL and Really Simple and watch the K.I.S.S. of The Good News of Jesus multiply throughout the globe!

About the Author

I became a born again Christian on September 18, 1988 one evening at a Pentecostal Church in Hurst, Texas. Prior to this moment in my life, I didn't know the Lord, or if there was a God. The way I saw it was that we were just left to our own devices in this life, to make the best of it. I was raised to believe that the bible was only a book that was applicable to those thousands of years ago that ran around with tents on their backs, and of no value for us in these days and times. Looking back over the course of my life, I learned that God always had people, and angels watching over me, and the only godly influence that I remember is an elderly couple, Mr. And Mrs. Walls who were my nannies during the first 12 years of my life. I truly believe that it was only an answer to their prayers over me that protected me from some very harmful events that I would walk through throughout my life prior to accepting the Lord into my life. Throughout the events in my life where I should have died, I believe that it was only by God's grace and Mr. and Mrs. Walls prayers that allowed me to live to the point in my life that I was ready to accept the Lord as my personal savior, and friend that sticks closer than a brother does. Here I must share with you the story of how I became born again that night during a church service.

My second husband had been telling me about God and Jesus, and that we needed to find a local church. Not that he believed that God could or would help him, but that I needed to find out for myself what God was all about. He instructed me to find an old time Pentecostal church where I would get the best dose of God he thought, and would find out what God was like. I spoke with the pastor of the church earlier in the week and he told me to tell my husband that we are exactly what he said to look for and please come and visit a Sunday service sometime. We went to the Sunday evening service that week, because my husband had said that would be where I would get the best dose of understanding of what God was about. As we entered the sanctuary of the church that night, I felt something very warm come over me. It was nothing like anything that I had ever felt before. We found a seat about in the middle row of the sanctuary, and sat down. Neither one of us said a word as the opening worship music played and then the preacher who was a visiting evangelist that evening began his sermon. I don't remember what the sermon was on, but I do remember what happened at the end of his sermon.

After he had finished his sermon, the music began to play again, and he begins to talk over the music. He tells all of us in the audience that if there was anyone here that would like to give their life to Jesus, when the singer beginning singing the first word of the song, please step forward, and come down front. All I remember is that I stood up, walked to the end of the row from where we were sitting, and the next thing I know, is that I am lying on the floor. Half way under the front row of pews in the sanctuary, and I am hearing my own words that I had spoken to a friend of mine back in High school being whispered into my right ear; "You told me that if I wanted you be believe in me that

I would have to come down here and meet you face to face and tell you that I am God." That night I believed and gave my heart to Jesus and was baptized the following weekend. An interesting Golden God Nugget about me telling you this part of my story is that I am actually writing this on September 18, 2011, exactly as God had instructed me, and when He told me to include this in the book. Dates and times are always significant with God, and He will see to it that your birthday is celebrated, as any parent will.

Not that I believe that everyone has to have such a radical conversion to Christ, however I believe that I had to have one since beginning at age 18 through the age of 21, I was addicted to drugs, and at the age of 20 I nearly died of a drug overdose, that my parents believed was postpartum depression. The only person that knew what was happening was my first husband at the time, and I believe if he hadn't given the drugs to bring me down, I would have died that night. Not that I recommend that you should self-medicate a person who is overdosing, but I am highlighting that drug users and abusers will self-medicate themselves and others in order to avoid the authorities that have the power to take their children away, or even send them to jail for using drugs.

Because I was suffering greatly from a Spirit of Rejection in my life, I didn't understand why I would go from one relationship to another relationship, looking for love in all the wrong places as the old country song goes, and never finding the peace, happiness, and love that I so desperately needed. A Spirit of Rejection can enter any one's life through the harmful soul ties of our dysfunctional families, physical, sexual or emotion abuse, the lack of love and appreciation for who God has created us to be, and through the harmful relationships that we will choose because of our lack of love for ourselves and others. Since the time that I accepted Jesus into my heart in 1988, He has continued his work of renewing my life, one fragment at a time. Freedom is a gradual process, and not an instant happening. Much like the slaves of years gone by, it takes a while for us to really accept that we are truly free from the bondages that once held us captive.

Since that time, I began teaching a bible study in my home in 1989, through that Pentecostal Church. I worked for another church, an Interdenominational church as their Director of the Bus Ministry, Pastoral Care Minister, Children's Pastor and Director of the Deliverance Ministry from 2003 to 2007, I graduated from Calvary Cathedral Bible College in 2007, then assigned to assist a new couple with getting their church started up. Then was called by God in 2008 to start my own ministry called Finally Free Ministries where we assist people who are coming out of a substance abuse or domestic violence situation. We provide this assistance with transitional housing, daycare assistance; jobs within our many businesses that have been started to support our ministry, life skills education and pastoral counseling.

Our long term goals are that we will build Mobile Home Park communities called Eddie's Acres across the United States beginning in Parker County Texas. We have estimated that it will cost approximately one million dollars to build each park to house 40 families or individuals enrolled in our programs with an on-site daycare facility that will provide quality childcare to those residents and will serve the community. The average yearly cost will be approximately one million per year to operate each facility, which will be funded through the multiple business ventures that Finally Free Ministries generate.

People wonder why I am so candid and open about my life. It is because of the love that My Father God has for me, that He has protected, and redeemed me and the things in my life to make me the Righteousness of God through what Jesus Christ my Lord and savior has done for me. I must testify of the things that God has brought me through, so that you too can know that God is no respecter of persons, and will heal, redeem and make you the Righteousness of God in Christ just as He has done for me! I call my candidness me taking my medicine, so that the skeletons of my past life don't pile up in the closet of my mind and keep me hostage to them. God has set me Finally Free, and He will do the same for any of you.